Presidential Stories: A Different Kind of Devotional

By Timothy D. Holder

TDH Communications

Knoxville, TN.

Cover art by Dan Lyle.

All Scripture quotations except one were taken from the Christian Standard Bible®, Copyright © 2017 by Holman Bible Publishers. Used by permission. Christian Standard Bible®, and CSB® are federally registered trademarks of Holman Bible Publishers. The Scripture quotation for Day 74 was taken from the King James Version of the Bible

ISBN-13 978-1727631500
ISBN-10 1727631501

Acknowledgements

Some time ago a friend gave me some advice. The friend, Jeff Bohanan, is a president in his own right—he owns an engineering and manufacturing company in East Tennessee called "Protomet." Knowing of my past work on US Presidents, and my faith in Christ, Jeff encouraged me to write a devotional, using Scripture of course, and telling stories about the Presidents to illustrate my points. I did not really catch the vision at first, but Jeff was persistent, so I decided to give it a try.

It was strange for me to take someone else's advice on what kind of writing project to do. Getting a book done is a tremendous amount of work, so it takes a lot of passion on my part. Usually when people suggest what I should write about, it is more of a reflection on their interests than mine. But here we are: The work is finished, and to be honest I have never enjoyed the actual process of writing more than I have with this book. Given my interests, it really was the perfect project for me. So, thank you, Jeff. I would not have done this without your continued encouragement.

I have little to no aptitude for the visual arts, so I am extremely grateful to Dan Lyle for his work on the cover. He brought talent, vision, and a gracious spirit to the project. He also had great ideas about some formatting issues.

There were people who offered editorial input, and I greatly appreciate their involvement. The aforementioned Jeff Bohanan and Dan Lyle had some helpful suggestions. Additionally, Judy Holder and Kay Brown read each devotion and offered editorial comments. What was so beneficial about their help was they tended to focus on different issues, making both of them invaluable. The time they sacrificed, their attention to detail, and the quality of their comments were all more helpful to me than I can say. And they did not just spot problems, they offered solutions.

There is another group of people who deserve acknowledgement: my, um, title advisors. I've written multiple books that have two-word titles beginning with *Presidential*. It made sense for me to do that with this book, too, but I couldn't quite nail it down. I solicited input from individuals who are all people of faith, who like history, are interested in writing, know something about marketing, or possess multiples of these characteristics. Thus, I offer my warmest thanks to Angela Holder, Baylee Bohanan, Jeff Bohanan, Kay Brown, Micki Duncan, Ryan Fogg, Kristin Haney, and Jonathan Hodge. If you like the title of the book, dear reader, you can thank this team for being part of the process. If you don't like it, be grateful to them anyway because I would have come up with something worse on my own.

I owe a thank you to Mike Nicely for being so committed to the idea of me getting a book done in 2018.

Finally, I'd would like to thank Angela Holder for her support, encouragement, and all around wonderfulness.

And to you, dear reader, I hope you get as much out of reading this book as I did writing it.

How to use this Book

Pray before you read it. Ask for wisdom. And then...

There are several different methods you might pursue. You could read one devotional a day until you reach the end; there are enough for about three months. You could read it just on the weekends, and use a different devotional during the week in which case it would take you about a year. You could flip that idea and read the devotional during the week then read something else on the weekends. The benefit of mixing it up is that sometimes variety helps keep us out of a rut.

You could read it by President by picking a President a day and reading all of his entries. This would lead to some uneven devotional experiences, though, because I have many more entries about some Presidents than others. Let's face it, the life of George Washington is a lot more interesting than that of Millard Fillmore.

Finally, as long as I am giving you unsolicited advice, I will offer one more bit. A lot of times when Christians offer up public prayer requests, and especially as we get a little more, um, seasoned in life, we tend to focus on health concerns. Often times, these requests are for loved ones, sometimes people we barely know, and sometimes for ourselves. Certainly, it is worthwhile to pray about these topics. But I would encourage you to also pray for things that will help equip you for the work to which you have been called. Pray for wisdom, love for others, and zeal for the Lord. Pray for your enemies. Pray for the lost and hurting people you know.

Author's Note

This book is organized by the dates of the stories, but I did not start at the beginning and write through to the end. I jumped here and there, as I inserted the stories in the book chronologically. I did not remember or discover the stories in order from start to finish.

Here's why this is so interesting to me: Several times there would be a common or similar theme between two stories that appear close to each other in the book even though I might have written and inserted them months apart in my writing process. In other words, I did not arrange this work by themes, but at times, it looks like Someone else did. That's pretty cool.

I hope you find *Presidential Stories* to be a useful tool in your growth as a disciple.

List of Devotions by Dates

34. May 10, Theodore Roosevelt, I Corinthians 4:16
35. May 11, Grover Cleveland, Psalm 139:14
36. May 16, Andrew Johnson, Proverbs 13:6
37. May 25, James Madison, Ecclesiastes 4:12
38. May 26, George Washington, I John 4:7
39. May 28, Andrew Jackson, John 13:34-35
40. May 29 James Polk, Judges 6:15-16
41. June 7, Thomas Jefferson, Proverbs 27:17
42. June 8A, Theodore Roosevelt, Psalm 19:1
43. June 8B, James Madison, Proverbs 19:21
44. June 11, George Washington, Matthew 18:15
45. June 12, Ronald Reagan, Galatians 2:11
46. June 14, Donald Trump, I Samuel 17:33
47. July 2, James Garfield, Psalm 116:12
48. July 4, Calvin Coolidge, Psalm 20:7
49. July 9, Zachary Taylor, Psalm 20:7
50. July 11, William Howard Taft, Judges 16:28A
51. July 17, John Adams, Thomas Jefferson, George Washington, I Peter 2:12
52. July 24, Bill Clinton and John Kennedy, I Corinthians 11:1
53. July 27, Dwight Eisenhower, Philippians 4:7
54. July 28, George Washington, Isaiah 6:8
55. July 31, Ulysses Grant, Matthew 7:5
56. August 2, Warren Harding, Ephesians 5:15-16
57. August 8, Richard Nixon, Romans 3:23
58. August 9, Gerald Ford, Colossians 3:12
59. August 12, Calvin Coolidge, Matthew 17: 20B
60. August 18, George H.W. Bush, Matthew 5:37
61. August 20, Benjamin Harrison, Psalm 139:14
62. August 24, James Madison, Deuteronomy 31:6
63. August 25, William McKinley, Matthew 10:16
64. September 6, William McKinley, Romans 12:12
65. September 11, George W. Bush, Psalm 30:5
66. September 19, George Washington, Deuteronomy 34:7
67. September 20, Chester Arthur, Luke 9:23
68. October 2, Harry Truman, Galatians 6:5

69. October 11, Jimmy Carter, Colossians 3:9
70. October 19, George Washington, Colossians 4:2
71. October 24, Herbert Hoover and Franklin Roosevelt, James 1:22
72. October 27, Theodore Roosevelt, Luke 6:40
73. October 30, John Adams, Romans 12:18
74. November 2A, Andrew Jackson, Proverbs 18:24
75. November 2B, James K. Polk, II Corinthians 5:17
76. November 4, Abraham Lincoln, Proverbs 31:25
77. November 5, Abraham Lincoln, Proverbs 22:13
78. November 11, Woodrow Wilson, Isaiah 9:6
79. November 12, George Washington, Matthew 25:21
80. November 19, James Garfield, Matthew 28:19
81. November 22A, John Kennedy, I Corinthians 3:5-7
82. November 22B, Lyndon Johnson, Matthew 14:28-30
83. November 23, Franklin Pierce, I Corinthians 9:24
84. December 2, Theodore Roosevelt, Isaiah 40:31
85. December 5, Martin Van Buren, John 5:17
86. December 7, Franklin Roosevelt, Esther 7:10
87. December 14, George Washington, Joshua 1:1
88. December 22, Andrew Jackson, Luke 23:34
89. December 25, Benjamin Harrison, Franklin Pierce, Luke 2:6-7
90. December 28, Thomas Jefferson, I Peter 5:6-7

List of Devotions by President

1. George Washington: February 10, March 17, April 13, April 29, May 6, May 26, June 11, July 17, July 28, September 19, October 19, November 12, December 14
2. John Adams: July 17, October 30
3. Thomas Jefferson: April 13, June 7, July 17, December 28
4. James Madison: May 25, June 8, August 24
5. James Monroe: February 16, April 28
6. John Quincy Adams: February 23, March 9
7. Andrew Jackson: May 28, November 2A, December 22
8. Martin Van Buren: March 4, December 5
9. William Henry Harrison: February 9
10. John Tyler: April 2
11. James Polk: May 29, November 2B
12. Zachary Taylor: July 9,
13. Millard Fillmore: January 7
14. Franklin Pierce: November 23, December 25
15. James Buchanan: January 4
16. Abraham Lincoln: January 1, April 9, April 14, May 7, November 4, November 5
17. Andrew Johnson: April 14, May 16,
18. Ulysses Grant: July 31, April 9
19. Rutherford Hayes: March 18
20. James Garfield: July 2, November 19
21. Chester Arthur: September 20,
22. Grover Cleveland: May 11
23. Benjamin Harrison: August 20, December 25
24. Grover Cleveland: May 11
25. William McKinley: August 25, September 6

Theodore Roosevelt: January 17, February 14, May 10, June 8, October 27, December 2

26. William Howard Taft: March 1, July 11
27. Woodrow Wilson: January 6, March 19, November 11
28. Warren Harding: August 2
29. Calvin Coolidge: July 4, August 12

30. Herbert Hoover: October 24
31. Franklin Roosevelt: April 12, October 24, December 7
32. Harry Truman: October 2
33. Dwight Eisenhower: March 28, July 27
34. John Kennedy: July 24, November 22A
35. Lyndon Johnson: November 22B
36. Richard Nixon: January 9, August 8
37. Gerald Ford: August 9, January 19
38. Jimmy Carter: October 11
39. Ronald Reagan: March 10, April 1, June 12
40. George H.W. Bush: January 6B, April 18, August 18
41. Bill Clinton: April 18, July 24
42. George W. Bush: September 11
43. Barack Obama: January 20
44. Donald Trump: January 20, June 1

Presidential Stories:

A Different Kind of Devotional

By Timothy D. Holder

Day 1

January 1

Isaiah 43:19A "Look, I am about to do something new; even now it is coming. Do you not see it?"

Abraham Lincoln

Republican Party

Embrace the Next Mission

New Year's Day is a time for beginning things. Abraham Lincoln became the first Republican president in the Election of 1860, but before he was a Republican, Lincoln was a Whig. The Whigs had a nice run, providing the country with 4 out of 5 Presidents at one stretch in American history. But the Whig Party was torn apart in the 1850s over the issue of slavery.

When the Whigs collapsed, Lincoln could have gotten discouraged and dropped out of politics. He could have been distracted and lamented what was lost, instead he made the transition to the Republican Party. The leaders in the party saw his gifts, he received the party nomination, and won the general election in 1860.

We have all lost things that were important to us. Sometimes we get paralyzed by that. We get frustrated over the unfairness of it, and we can't stop looking backwards. But we run the risk of missing out on God's blessings in the present and the future, if our minds and hearts are focused on the past.

We need to recognize that the things of this world are temporary. It's a blessing to cherish good memories, but as doors close, we need to step into the next calling God has for us. What new person or project is God guiding us towards? For some of us, it is time to let go of the past and embrace the new mission.

Day 2

January 4

I Thessalonians 5:17 "Pray constantly."

James Buchanan

Democratic Party

Prayer

James Buchanan declared January 4, 1861 a national day of fasting, humiliation, and prayer. That sounds like a great thing for a President to do, though we might be a little iffy today on the humiliation part. Back then, it meant more like a time for humility.

While all of this is good, there is a truth that is hard to avoid as a historian or as a Christian: Buchanan is considered by many to be one of the worst Presidents ever. Some historians say he was the worst.

Spoiler alert: most of these devotions are going to be positive. But Buchanan was something else. He even drove James Polk crazy when Buchanan was Polk's secretary of state, so at least Buchanan was consistent.

The reality is that most of us have a little James Buchanan inside of us. We face situations, and sometimes we're just not good enough, smart enough, or wise enough. Do we at least have the wisdom of James Buchanan to look to prayer at some point? Do we treat prayer like a lucky rabbit's foot? Do we go to it as a last resort without really putting a lot of stock in it?

Too often we talk about how great prayer is, but we don't actually pray.

Let us pray without ceasing today.

Day 3

January 6A

I John 4:8 "The one who does not love does not know God, because God is love."

Woodrow Wilson

Democratic Party

Racism

Our 28th President, Woodrow Wilson, has the reputation of being a devout Christian, and he did graduate work in the field of history, so he must have been a man of rare quality and refinement, right?

Okay, seriously, Woodrow Wilson was a Christian and historian who was heavily influenced by his father's Christian faith and love of history. But Wilson also latched onto his father's belief that it was okay to treat African Americans badly in comparison to whites. On January 6, 1861 Woodrow Wilson's father preached a sermon about how slavery is biblical.

Our kids are susceptible to acquiring the prejudices and biases that we display, so we need to be careful. By the same token, we might—possibly without fully realizing it—display a prejudice based on race or gender that we picked up during our own childhood.

Some sins can be generational.

With prayer, and by the power of the Holy Spirit, we can break the cycle. We must break this cycle. How can we communicate a Gospel of love to a dying and desperate world, if we have created mental and social barriers based on a personal characteristic, like race, that people have no control over? Some of us need to be willing to change and grow.

Day 4

January 6B

Mark 10:9 "Therefore what God has joined together, let no one separate."

George H.W. Bush

Republican Party

Marriage

On this day in 1945, George and Barbara Bush got married. Their 72 years together gave them the longest marriage of any presidential couple. Marriage can present one with many trials. Bush spent almost a year as Director of the CIA, and he was a leader of the Republican Party during the Watergate Scandal, so secrets and job-related stress played a significant role in his life. Such things can destroy marriages, but as the Bushes demonstrated, it is possible to spend one's life devoted to a single spouse. Many marriages end in failure. Many other couples don't get divorced, but it would be wrong to describe what they have as a success.

Those of us who are Christians and married have an obligation to demonstrate what a blessing marriage can be. That might sound like a guilt-inducing or frustrating idea for someone who is struggling in an unhappy marriage. There is no easy, magical, bullet-proof advice for turning around a failing relationship. But there are some key ingredients: prayer, a forgiving heart, Biblically-based counseling, and a whole lot of patience.

Obviously, it is easier to write a list than fix a broken marriage, but we can't get to the end of the journey without taking the necessary steps. The list provides the tools; it does not rebuild the house.

Some marriages seem beyond repair, but have you ever heard of a couple that gets a divorce, then they remarry each other? I have. (True story: It was Marie Osmond.)

There are some readers who do not need this devotional message today. Maybe for those of us who are in a good place, we are supposed to take this message and encourage someone else with it.

Day 5

January 7

I Corinthians 10:31 "So, whether you eat or drink or whatever you do, do everything for the glory of God."

Millard Fillmore

Whig Party

Work Hard

On this day in the year 1800, Millard Fillmore was born, which might seem kind of insignificant. A lot of Americans through the ages have been named after Washington and Jefferson, and more recently after Reagan and Kennedy, but who among us has ever met a Millard?

He's President #13, which sounds unlucky, if you believe in that sort of thing. I don't. In a universe ruled by a loving and logical God, why would a random number increase someone's chance of misfortune? It doesn't make sense to me, but we are getting off topic.

Fillmore didn't actually get elected, he just took over after Zachary Taylor died unexpectedly. So, Fillmore is pretty obscure today, but at the time, he was the most well-known man in America. He might not have been elected President, but he was successful enough to be chosen for the second seat, and he was our Chief Executive for more than two and a half years. He was successful by just about any fair metric one would use to judge him.

Could 5% of Americans today give one fact about Fillmore, other than that he was President? Would 5% of Americans today remember him at all? His achievements and successes did not withstand the test of time.

We need to devote ourselves to things that matter.

Am I saying that Fillmore's career of public service doesn't matter? I am absolutely not saying that.

Because of our jobs, we provide for our families and support our local churches and missions. For most of us, our place of work is our primary mission field. Our jobs are important because if we are mediocre at work, it diminishes our witness. We need to work hard and smart, but for many of us the work is not the goal; it is a means to an end. We work to honor and glorify God.

Day 6

January 9

I Corinthians 13:4A "Love is patient, love is kind."

Richard Nixon

Republican Party

Love

Richard Nixon opened his eyes to the world on this day in 1913. He did a lot of things that prepared him well for the presidency. Born in California, he went to law school in North Carolina then got a job in Washington DC in the federal government. He could have avoided military service because of his pacifistic religious beliefs (he was a Quaker), but joined anyway after Pearl Harbor was attacked.

When World War Two ended, Nixon got elected to the House of Representatives and later the Senate before serving two terms as the VP for Dwight Eisenhower. There were times when Ike dealt with serious health issues, and Nixon essentially served as the acting President.

Despite all of that, Nixon's presidency ended in failure when he resigned in disgrace over the Watergate scandal. I am convinced (for reasons that are too lengthy to fully explain here) that Nixon was done in partially by his poor relationships with those who worked for him. Nixon swayed a bunch of voters across the land, but he was too cold to connect with the people working for him. As a result, his people tried to connect with him by doing whatever it took to succeed. It was the only way to win Nixon's favor.

Some of us have had great successes and accomplishments, but are we communicating love to people, or are we too focused on getting things done? As Christians we are called to be relational. We should pray about that today in whatever circumstances we find ourselves.

Day 7

January 17

Matthew 20: 26B "On the contrary, whoever wants to become great among you must be your servant."

Theodore Roosevelt

Republican Party

Be Servant-Minded

Benjamin Franklin was born on this day in 1706. He was not a President of course. If you thought he was, I'm not disappointed, I just look at it as job security for me.

Some historians say Franklin invented bifocals, but today's devotion is not about Franklin or bifocals, it is about a President with a vision problem.

Theodore Roosevelt liked to push himself physically, and he was a fan of boxing. He liked to spar with professional boxers and just about anybody else who would put up his fists. One day in 1908, Roosevelt was sparring with a young military officer who was part of the White House guard detail. The younger man landed a blow against the side of Roosevelt's head, and the President went permanently blind in one eye. Roosevelt stopped the fight immediately, which is hardly a shock. What is remarkable, though, is that Roosevelt never told the young man what happened, because the President was concerned the younger man would be devastated by what he had done.

The President's concern for the officer's feelings in the midst of Roosevelt's own pain and loss is amazing. We should aspire to such a level of compassion today.

Day 8

January 19

John 14:12 "Truly I tell you, the one who believes in me will do the works that I do. And he will do even greater works than these, because I am going to the Father."

Gerald Ford

Republican Party

Dream Big

This date in 1977 was Gerald Ford's last full day as President of the United States. He lost the Election of 1976, which meant Jimmy Carter was taking over. Running for the presidency was something Ford would not have anticipated doing even just a few years before this. Despite being a career politician in D.C., Ford had never dreamed of being President. His ambition after many years in the House of Representatives was to become Speaker someday. This could only happen if his Republican Party won a majority in the House and then his peers chose him to be their leader.

By the time the 1970s arrived, Ford saw that his chance to be Speaker had pretty much evaporated. When Nixon's first VP, Spiro Agnew, resigned in disgrace over corruption not related to Watergate, Ford was picked to replace him. Then Nixon resigned, and Ford became President without ever running on a national ticket. Every other President was elected by voters across the nation as President or VP. Ford took the most powerful job in the free world without getting a vote from outside his home state of Michigan.

Once in office, the man who had never dreamed of being President discovered he liked the job, felt he was pretty good at it, and decided to run in 1976 to get four more years.

Ford got something bigger than he ever dreamed of, and sometimes God works that way in our lives, too. Why are our dreams so small when our God is so big? We should dream big today about how God might use us for His glory.

Day 9

January 20

Romans 12:18 "If possible, as far as it depends on you, live at peace with everyone."

Barack Obama

Democratic Party

Donald Trump

Republican Party

Peace

Barack Obama and Donald Trump are not really mutual fans, but for one day, they were able to share something with each other that was pretty special: the presidency. On this day in 2017, Obama started out as President, then Trump was sworn into office and took over.

One of the great things about our country is that even when people don't like the election results, even when people angrily say, "I didn't vote for him; he's not *my* President," we have generally peaceful elections. The losing party gives up the White House without violence.

How do we handle it when we don't get our way? Are we able to sit together with people whose values we don't share, like the Obamas and Trumps did on Inauguration Day? Can we demonstrate the love of Christ and be the peacemakers He called us to be in His Sermon on the Mount?

If we do what the Bible says today and love our enemies, it sure would make it easier to get along.

Day 10

February 9

James 4:14 "Yet you do not know what tomorrow will bring—what your life will be! For you are like a vapor that appears for a little while, then vanishes."

William Henry Harrison

Whig Party

Time

On this day in 1773, William Henry Harrison was born. He is most well-known for having the shortest presidency, since he died just one month after his inauguration.

The story goes that he got sick on Inauguration Day because he gave a long speech in unseasonably cold weather. He got progressively worse and died. Harrison blamed his declining condition on the endless horde of office seekers bothering him at all hours of the day. He said he didn't have time to get better because people would not leave him alone.

Harrison died because he was a sick older man in an era when a lot of medical ideas were terrible, not primarily because he was too busy to rest. But sometimes we use the same rationale for what plagues us. I'd get in shape/get more involved in church/be a better spouse/be a better parent/pray more/read my Bible with regularity/get more sleep, if I just had the time.

God in His infinite wisdom gives us 7 days a week and 24 hours a day. We have time, we have opportunities, and we have consequences. We will not get extra hours in a day, or extra days in the week, so there is no need to waste our time praying for those things. We should pray that we will be better stewards of the time God has allotted us.

Day 11

February 10

I Peter 1:14 "As obedient children, do not be conformed to the desires of your former ignorance."

George Washington

No Political Party Affiliation

Impulse Control

On this day in 1763, the Treaty of Paris was signed, formally ending the French and Indian War. It was called the 7 Years' War in Europe (because, well, it lasted seven years), but fighting in America actually started two years earlier. A central figure from the start was a young Virginian named George Washington. It is commonly pointed out by historians that Washington gained valuable experience in this war which helped him lead American forces during the Revolutionary War several years later. He led forces from the Virginia militia and was briefly attached to the staff of a British general.

There were two lessons Washington learned which he really did not appreciate: the "Indian style" of fighting and the virtues of knowing when to avoid battle.

Washington admired the discipline that characterized the British method of volley-fire shooting. Yet that highly-structured, European style, featuring long rows of men engaged in orderly and simultaneous firing, was not as effective in the New World as it was in the Old. The Native Americans were much more efficient with their use of concealment, fast movement, and hit and run attacks. Washington was also a naturally aggressive man who preferred rushing in and fighting as opposed to avoiding battle until the odds were in his favor. Washington did not want to bend on these two ideas, the superiority of European-style fighting and always jumping into battle at the earliest opportunity, but he ultimately did. The tall Virginian prioritized success over his personal preferences.

We need to be willing to learn from experience and control our impulses. We can serve God more effectively when we sacrifice our pride and stubbornness at the foot of the Cross.

Day 12

February 14

Romans 12:15 "Rejoice with those who rejoice, weep with those who weep."

Theodore Roosevelt

Republican Party

Empathy

Have you ever had a bad Valentine's Day? Theodore Roosevelt had a worse one. His beloved young wife and his almost equally beloved mother both died on February 14, 1884 in his house. His little daughter lost her mother and her grandmother. He was distraught and broken, but he did not passively wallow in misery. He decided he needed to do something active and get away. He moved to North Dakota and lived the rough and dangerous life of a cowboy for three years. It was a very Teddy Roosevelt thing to do.

I have had some wonderful Valentine's Days with my wife, and I had several lonely ones before I met her. Every year I am surrounded by people living in both extremes. Sometimes on big days we get so caught up in our own business we might get a little oblivious to others. If you are having a great Valentine's Day, don't forget to have a little love and sensitivity for those who feel alone. If you are not currently in a romantic relationship, don't reduce Valentine's Day to just that. Focus on love in general. Celebrate and love the people God has put in your orbit.

Make the extra effort to focus outward.

Day 13

February 16

James 2:26 "For just as the body without the spirit is dead, so also faith without works is dead."

James Monroe

Democratic-Republican Party

Spiritual Fruit

On this day in 1786, James Monroe married his beloved wife, Elizabeth. What makes this interesting is the ceremony would have been a religious one. Having a marriage officiated by a minister is hardly rare of course, but it might have been a rare occasion for Monroe in this regard: Several historians consider him to be one of the least religious of all the American Presidents.

Do we know conclusively that Monroe was not a believer? No, we do not, but it is interesting that several different historians rate Monroe the same. Majority opinion could be wrong, but we are known by our fruit, and apparently not much of Monroe's spiritual fruit survived the test of time, if there was much to start with.

Monroe was a popular and successful President and a legitimate hero after fighting in the American Revolution, and helping guide military policy as a member of James Madison's Cabinet during the War of 1812. But if we want a hero of the faith, we will have to look elsewhere.

This begs a question for us, though: If our lives were examined as extensively as James Monroe's has been, would our spiritual fruit be visible? Other than maybe going to church and not cussing (much…in public), how are our lives different because of our faith?

"Faith without works is dead."

Did we look spiritually dead yesterday?

What are we going to do about it today?

Day 14

February 23

I Thessalonians 5:17 "Pray constantly."

John Quincy Adams

Democratic-Republican Party

Prayer

John Quincy Adams died on this date in 1848, and the nation lost a brilliant man and a committed public servant. Adams was certainly well-qualified to be our sixth President.

He was a renowned diplomat—George Washington thought Adams was in a class by himself, and one of Washington's many gifts was an ability to recognize quality individuals. Adams' greatest achievement as a diplomat was helping to hammer out the peace treaty that ended the War of 1812.

Adams was also a state senator in Massachusetts, a US senator, and secretary of state for James Monroe.

Despite all of that governmental and diplomatic experience, Adams was an unsuccessful and unpopular President. The reasons don't matter here, but my point does: Sometimes all the experience and expertise in the world won't help you get the job done, so don't take any chances—pray a lot…about everything.

Don't just read those words and move on. Seriously: Pray a lot…about everything. You might have noticed that this, the 14th devotion, has the same Scripture and point as your second devotion did. You will get no apology here. Some messages we need to hear more than once.

If you have lived out this message since your read it earlier, then the point of you reading it today was to urge you to share the message with someone who needs to hear it. You will most likely be surrounded by such people.

Please note: This will not be a book characterized by an overabundance of repeated themes. Prayer is just particularly important for us.

Day 15

March 4

Proverbs 11:2 "When arrogance comes, disgrace follows, but with humility comes wisdom."

Martin Van Buren

Democratic Party

Humility

On this day in 1837, Martin Van Buren took office as President. The year he entered the White House, the federal government actually took in more money than it spent, and politicians were trying to figure out what to do with the surplus. Before Van Buren left office after his one term, a terrible depression had hit, which led to a landslide by the Whig Party in the next presidential election. Van Buren was the 8th President, and he was the first one not named "Adams" to get rejected by the voters in his reelection bid.

Sometimes it is easy to get a little cocky or complacent when we're in the midst of easy times or we've experienced a little success. Our victories and our assets can be fleeting things, a vapor of smoke. We would do well to stop, take a breath, and put our trust in the Lord, not in our circumstances.

Martin Van Buren was a shrewd political operative. He had served as secretary of state and VP under Andrew Jackson, and his loyalty paid off when the Democrats chose Van Buren to lead the way. Then things went sideways, and people started calling him "Martin Van Ruin," which is kind of funny now, but it is a little brutal.

We hit highs and lows in life. We would do well to stay humble in our victories.

Day 16

March 8

Philippians 4:6 "Don't worry about anything, but in everything, through prayer and petition with thanksgiving, present your requests to God."

William Howard Taft

Republican Party

Stress

On this day in 1930, William Howard Taft passed away. Sadly for Taft, even though he reached the lofty height of President of the United States, the only thing most people know about him is he got stuck in a bathtub. Some question if this actually happened, but the story behind the story makes the incident believable enough. Taft was a guy who struggled with his weight long before facing the pressure of the presidency. After his inauguration, he took stress eating to a whole new level. He ended up in the 340-350 lb. range, which is especially remarkable given that people tended to be lighter 100 years ago than we are today (nowadays we eat bigger portions, more sugar, and fattier foods, but I digress).

Taft couldn't handle his stress and turned to food for comfort. Many Christians today do the same thing. Or, we have some other vice, some other obsession, some other sin in which we indulge. When stressed, we need to turn to Christ. When the stress returns, we need to turn to Christ again. This isn't about losing weight (primarily), many of us struggle with vices that are just as destructive if not more so. This is about going to Christ for comfort instead of distracting ourselves with something less worthy.

Day 17

March 9

Hebrews 6:19A "We have this hope as an anchor for the soul."

John Quincy Adams

Democratic-Republican Party

Hope

On this day in 1841, the former 6th President of the United States, John Quincy Adams, argued on behalf of Africans who were in danger of being sent into slavery. These individuals had been on a slave ship called the *Amistad*. They had overcome their captors, and made their way to America, but their problems were not over.

Given that slavery still existed in the United States, racism was rampant, and there was an overseas slave trade that was illegal but still profitable, there were many who wanted the *Amistad* passengers to not be free. A legal battle ensued, and it went all the way to the Supreme Court.

John Quincy Adams' four unpopular and unhappy years as President had ended in early 1829. He probably felt there were no more major contributions he could make to history. But he fought for the freedom of the *Amistad* passengers and argued their cause before the United States Supreme Court. The Court ruled in favor of Adams, and the Africans were freed.

The popular phrase "hope is not a strategy" is true, but hope can be an anchor. We can stand fast and believe that while we probably won't argue a case before the Supreme Court, if we are breathing, we are still being called to do something for the Kingdom of God. It is our responsibility to go and do today. Certain opportunities might have passed by, but the Lord still has a purpose for us.

Day 18

March 10

Colossians 4:18A "I, Paul, am writing this greeting with my own hand."

Ronald Reagan

Republican Party

Steps of Faith

On this day in 1947, Ronald Reagan was elected President...of the Screen Actors' Guild. Reagan was nominated *in absentia*, but he was interested in the position because he was concerned about Communists trying to infiltrate Hollywood.

Some readers might see that as paranoid today, others might be thinking, "Yeah, and the Communists succeeded." More significant for this devotional is what Reagan's move did in his life. Getting a taste of leadership and the opportunity to rally people to a cause prompted Reagan to take more steps in a political direction. He later became the Governor of California and was eventually the 40th President of the United States.

One important step can take us to another we don't yet anticipate. When we are faithful, we might be taken to areas and opportunities of impact that will amaze us!

The Apostle Paul realized he had to stop persecuting Christians. But in that moment he had no idea he would end up going on long missionary journeys to speak on behalf of Christ, much less end up writing a significant chunk of the New Testament.

We need to be faithful to what we are called to do today. Who knows where the next step of faith might lead?

Day 19

March 17

Psalm 33:8 "Let the Whole Earth fear the Lord; let all the inhabitants of the world stand in awe of Him."

George Washington

No Political Party Affiliation

Awe

Happy St. Patrick's Day! On days like today, or when Notre Dame has an upset win in football, there are those who like to talk about "the luck of the Irish." I don't, but some people do.

One person who people might call lucky was George Washington. On a cold night when he was a teenager, he was sleeping outside on a bed of straw, which caught on fire, but someone woke him up in time to not get burned to death. Another time, he was in a one-day battle during the French and Indian War. On that day, he had two horses got shot out from under him, and he ended up with four bullet holes in his jacket, but he was uninjured. Additionally, in the American Revolution Washington and some soldiers came under such heavy gunfire from the British that they literally disappeared in the gun smoke. One of Washington's officers was so sure the general was dead, the man buried his face in his hat. When the smoke cleared, once again Washington was in unharmed.

Is luck really a thing? I don't believe so. I do believe, though, that the Creator of the universe sometimes chooses to intervene. God doesn't serve us; we serve Him. But sometimes He chooses to get involved in human affairs, and the fact that He can and does move in our lives should give us a sense of awe today.

Day 20

March 18

John 3:16 "For God loved the world in this way: He gave His one and only Son, so that everyone who believes in Him will not perish but have eternal life."

Rutherford Hayes

Republican Party

The Mercy of Christ

On this day in 1892, Rutherford Hayes said something profound. "I commit my soul to the mercy of God through our Lord Jesus Christ." If you are reading a book like this, and you have gotten this far into it, there's a pretty good chance you have made such a commitment with your soul, too. But it is good for those of us who are in Christ to stop every now and again and remind ourselves of this commitment. We need to re-orient ourselves to what ultimately matters. We can be so tempted to put our peace of mind in our circumstances when we really just need to put our trust in the mercy of God that Hayes talks about.

Hayes was the first to admit that he did not have all the answers to the theological and denominational questions of his day, but he found his peace in the mercy of God.

His election to the White House was a real mess—imagine Florida in the year 2000...times 3 (3 times the states, not 3 times the year 2000—that wouldn't make sense). In the Election of 1876, the voting results were disputed in 3 states that all ended up going to Hayes. If any of the 3 had gone to his opponent, Hayes would have lost, and you wouldn't know his name today.

What should have been a year of celebration of the centennial of the United States was instead a highly contentious time when people were talking about another Civil War.

In the end, the political parties made a deal and moved past the dispute, but it serves as a reminder that life can get filled with drama and tension. We can keep things in perspective by relying on the mercy of Christ.

Day 21

March 19

Colossians 3:23 "Whatever you do, do it from the heart, as something done for the Lord and not for people."

Woodrow Wilson

Democratic Party

Work

On this day in 1860, William Jennings Bryan was born. If you're tempted to ask, "Which number President was William Jennings Bryan?" don't. He wasn't a President. He ran for the office thrice, and lost each time, but that's not why I'm writing about him.

He was the secretary of state for Woodrow Wilson, and that became a problem. Wilson was walking a tightrope as he sought re-election in 1916. He had only won a plurality of the popular vote in 1912, meaning most of the voters wanted someone else. World War One started in 1914, and the nation was divided over it. Should we get involved or stay out? Wilson was trying to split the difference. As of 1915, we hadn't declared war, or otherwise committed ourselves militarily, but we were providing all kinds of material support to the Allies.

If two people you knew were in a fight, could you hand one of them a set of brass knuckles and a baseball bat, and still pretend you weren't taking sides?

As former President Theodore Roosevelt was going around the country demanding we get involved and calling Wilson a weakling, Secretary of State Bryan was saying we needed to be strictly neutral. Bryan eventually resigned because he could not support Wilson's policy.

If we can't support the goals of our organization, it is time to look for a new job. How can we do our work "from the heart," if we don't believe in what we're doing? Working as part of something we don't believe in might be easy on payday, but what about the rest of our days? It could be time to either change our attitude about our job, or look around for something else and pray.

Day 22

March 28

Luke 12:48B "From everyone who has been given much, much will be required, and from the one who has been entrusted with much, even more will be respected."

Dwight Eisenhower

Republican Party

Good Stewardship

This is the day in 1969 when Dwight Eisenhower died. It was a significant loss for America because he was quite a man.

One thing that makes Eisenhower a rarity is he, Zachary Taylor, and Donald Trump are the only Presidents to have never held a political office before becoming Chief Executive. Even George Washington had held a colonial office before there was a United States.

What gave Ike, as Eisenhower was known, the audacity to think he was qualified to be President? Well, there was this little thing called World War Two, and Ike was in charge of the European Theater, and it turned out pretty well.

What do you do for an encore after that?

Ike had learned how to handle a huge and meaningful undertaking, and he was looking for some other kind of significant work to do next. People started suggesting the presidency. Sometimes in life we pursue something because we are really excited about doing it. At other times, we need to be willing to do a thing because we have the skill set, and/or we have the resources and life experience to get it done. What project—maybe big and audacious, maybe kind of small in the eyes of others—has God prepared us for?

Is this our day to go and do?

Day 23

April 1

Ecclesiastes 3:4 "a time to weep and a time to laugh; a time to mourn and a time to dance."

Ronald Reagan

Republican Party

Humor

April Fool's Day is obviously a day devoted to efforts to have a good laugh. One of the things Ronald Reagan was known for was his sense of humor.

Reagan joked about big government, saying "The most terrifying words in the English language are: I'm from the government, and I'm here to help."

Part of what made his humor effective was that he did not just aim his barbs outward; he was willing to poke fun at himself. He joked about being old. "Thomas Jefferson once said, 'We should never judge a President by his age, only by his works.' And ever since he told me that, I stopped worrying," said Reagan.

Humor has a lot of upside. It can lighten the mood in a tense situation, or make a speech more interesting. It can help create a connection with people.

If we truly have the joy of the Lord, then laughter should be a part of the equation. Joyful people laugh easily.

Laughter doesn't always work. Obviously, there are seasons in life when we mourn, and some people use humor negatively—I have certainly been guilty of that. But an easy laugh can serve as proof of peace in our souls, and it can make us pleasant to be around.

How can we communicate joy today? Laughter is one such way.

Day 24

April 4

Galatians 6:7 "Don't be deceived: God is not mocked. For whatever a person sows he will also reap."

John Tyler

Whig Party

Consequences

When John Tyler took over for William Henry Harrison on this day in 1841, Tyler was a little ill-prepared. Harrison had only been in office for a month when he died, so there wasn't much time for either man to get up to speed.

It's possible, though, that all the time in the world would not have helped Tyler. He had only joined the Whig Party because he fell out with Andrew Jackson, at which point Tyler didn't want to be a Democrat any more. Once in power as the 10th President, Tyler alienated his fellow Whigs to the point that he was expelled from the party, but not before his entire Cabinet quit on him.

Tyler wasn't even on the ballot in 1844, because neither party wanted him. He went home to Virginia after James Polk took office, and once he was back home, his neighbors elected Tyler to be in charge of road maintenance. If that seems like a step down from being President of the United States, it was. If it seems like a bit of an insult, it was meant to be that, too.

Actions have consequences. Tyler didn't get along with people and he paid a price for that. As Christians, we should definitely stand up for our principles and beliefs, but some of us use our principles and beliefs as a pretext to act like jerks.

Goal for the day: Be strong, but don't be a jerk.

Day 25

April 9

Matthew 5:7 "Blessed are the merciful, for they will be shown mercy."

Abraham Lincoln

Republican Party

Ulysses Grant

Republican Party

Mercy of Christ

On this day in 1865, Robert E. Lee surrendered to Ulysses S. Grant, which for all practical purposes ended the Civil War. Grant would use this achievement as a springboard into two terms in the White House as he became the 18th President.

One of the knocks on Grant—other than the accusation that he was an alcoholic—was that he was too indifferent to the suffering of his men. They got slaughtered by the thousands during his military campaigns. Lincoln was under serious pressure to relieve Grant of duty, as body counts rose higher. But Lincoln held fast. The 16th President believed many of his generals were too timid. Grant was getting more men killed than other commanders, but he was also winning battles and gaining ground.

Grant's reputation makes his actions towards Lee's men pretty interesting. Grant did not order his forces to take Lee's army as prisoners, which might have been impractical anyway, given the large numbers involved. But Grant allowed the southern officers to keep their pistols, swords, and horses, which was surprisingly generous. Also, it would not have been out of the ordinary for the Union soldiers to, at minimum, loot the Confederates' personal possessions in an effort to claim mementos of the occasion, but Grant issued an order against such behavior.

Grant knew, and Lincoln did as well, that the best path forward to heal the nation required mercy. As we navigate our own conflicts in life, sometimes mercy is required from us. When we are tempted to think our enemies and rivals don't deserve mercy because of what they did to us, we would do well to remember we didn't deserve mercy either, but Christ gave it freely.

We are called to be like Christ.

Day 26

April 12

Philippians 3:13-14 "Brothers and sisters, I do not consider myself to have taken hold of it. But one thing I do: Forgetting what is behind and reaching forward to what is ahead, I pursue as my goal the prize promised by God's heavenly call in Christ Jesus."

Franklin Roosevelt

Democratic Party

Grit

On this day in 1945, Franklin Delano Roosevelt passed away. This occurred shortly after he began his unprecedented fourth term as president. Though Andrew Jackson and Grover Cleveland had won the popular vote 3 times, they only won the Electoral College twice. Many Presidents had been elected twice, but four times? That was extraordinary.

What was the secret to FDR's success? It was quite simple really. After he had served two terms, he kept running. A lot of times in life the secret to success is not primarily talent, it's grit. Do we keep going on the job when we get discouraged? Do we stay committed to our marriage when the times get tough? Do we rededicate ourselves to prayer and Bible study when our spiritual life gets stale? Do we choose to demonstrate the love of Christ when people aren't so lovable?

What is it today that is weighing us down? We need to keep going, keep praying, and not quit.

Day 27

April 13

Acts 15:39 "They (Paul and Barnabas) had such a sharp disagreement that they parted company, and Barnabas took Mark with him and sailed off to Cyprus."

Thomas Jefferson

Democratic-Republican Party

George Washington

No Political Party Affiliation

Grace

Thomas Jefferson was born on this day in 1743. His parents had no idea how famous he would become. There was no way they could know that he would write the Declaration of Independence or later become the 3rd President of the United States, which of course did not exist when Jefferson was born. Jefferson's parents could not know that at a point between the Declaration and the presidency, Thomas Jefferson would have a falling out with George Washington. Jefferson didn't like Washington's political philosophy, and Washington didn't like people who spread unkind rumors implying he was senile and then lying about it.

Yep, things got tense.

Like Paul and Barnabas before them, Washington and Jefferson were doing something great together, but they reached a point where they couldn't get along. We should learn from them.

Sometimes it's easier to forgive our enemies than it is to forgive our friends.

Goal for the day: Pray that we will show grace to those around us.

Day 28

April 14

Deuteronomy 32:35A "Vengeance belongs to Me; I will repay."

Abraham Lincoln

Republican Party

Andrew Johnson

Republican Party

Revenge

This was a sad day in American history in 1865 when Abraham Lincoln was shot by the Virginian John Wilkes Booth. After Lincoln died, many in the North were shocked and outraged by the evil deed.

In the long run, the South suffered more from the death of Lincoln than the North did. Lincoln became a lot more popular in death than he had ever been in life. For Yankees who had hard feelings towards the South because of all the northern dead and wounded from the war, the murder of Lincoln was the last straw. Northern politicians scored points with their constituents by doling out tough measures against the South.

Lincoln, a Midwestern northerner, had strongly advocated a milder form of Reconstruction than Congress ended up pursuing. Andrew Johnson, who became President upon Lincoln's death, also advocated milder reforms. But Johnson, a working-class southerner, was quickly dismissed as politically biased (and interpersonally irritating). Congress ran over Johnson like he wasn't even there.

John Wilkes Booth thought he was striking a great blow on behalf of the Confederacy. Really, though, he just outraged the North and hurt the South. Lashing out in anger can be tempting, and it might be satisfying in the moment. But there are consequences to such behavior.

We need to resist the impulse for revenge. The consequences can be devastating. There are some things we just need to leave in the hands of the Lord.

Day 29

April 18

Matthew 5:44 "But I tell you, love your enemies and pray for those who persecute you."

George H.W. Bush

Republican Party

Bill Clinton

Democratic Party

Loving our Enemies

On this day in 2018, there was an article about a professor in California who tweeted remarkably unkind things when news broke of Barbara Bush's death. The professor said the former First Lady was a racist who raised a war criminal. The professor went on to say she was "happy the witch was dead."

Bill Clinton had a different response. Though his politics, like those of the California professor, were different from those of the Bush family, Clinton offered nothing but kind words. It is unsurprising. Clinton became friends with George and Barbara Bush after the two former Presidents worked together on a humanitarian cause. The political rivals, who ran against each other in 1992, became friends.

How do we respond when someone we disagree with experiences a setback? Do we openly attack them? Do we stay silent while privately rejoicing in the misery of our enemies? We are called to something better. We are commanded to actually love them.

The arrangement of these devotions is driven by the dates of the events that are cited. Interestingly, we have had several within a short span that deal with love, grace, and forgiveness. It's almost as if we need to keep hearing the same kind of message over and over, because we lack charity in our hearts for those who have hurt us or have different views than we do. I do not believe this is coincidental at all.

Do we need to stop now and repent of an uncharitable attitude towards someone we find disagreeable?

Day 30

April 28

Philippians 4:8-9 "Finally brothers and sisters, whatever is true, whatever is honorable, whatever is just, whatever is pure, whatever is lovely, whatever is commendable—if there is any moral excellence and if there is anything praiseworthy—dwell on these things. Do what you have learned and received and heard from me, and seen in me, and the God of peace will be with you."

James Monroe

Democratic-Republican Party

Being Positive

If I were to tell you James Monroe, born on this day in 1758, was the second most popular President in American history, you might disagree. You might think my ranking of Monroe is just my opinion. But it is not—I can back it up with science. Okay, not science exactly, but I can give you some interesting data. George Washington got every single electoral vote in two elections. Nobody else can claim that, but Monroe was almost as impressive. When he had served four years, then ran for reelection, he got every electoral vote but one—almost as good as Washington.

Was Monroe really that special? Well, he was, as mentioned previously in this book, a war hero, fighting and getting wounded during the Revolution. And he was secretary of war during the War of 1812, which was kind of a big deal, since he was the only man in Madison's Cabinet who knew anything about how to actually conduct a war.

What really helped Monroe was that the Federalist Party was collapsing, so there was no organized opposition. But still, every vote but one is pretty impressive.

Monroe was almost the unanimous choice in his reelection, but no one puts him on their short list of great presidents today. Here's the thing, though: Probably nobody who would diminish Monroe today has had as much impact on America as he did during his lifetime. There are two types of people in this world: There are those who sit on the sidelines and tear down people who do stuff, and those who actually do stuff.

Which kind of people are we? Let's go out today and focus more on doing something positive, rather than just saying something negative.

Day 31

April 29

I Corinthians 15:33 "Do not be deceived: Bad company corrupts good morals."

George Washington

No Party Affiliation

Peer Pressure

On this day in 2018, a former student of mine, Brett Reed, walked into my office and gave me card that included the quotation from George Washington "It is better to be alone than in bad company." The student was using this to explain why he had been refusing to meet with me.

Just kidding.

Anyway, the quotation is interesting because many adults tend to think of peer pressure as something that primarily impacts kids. The reality is we are pretty much all in some kind of peer group (unless we are isolating ourselves), and/or we are in the employ of somebody. We can face all kinds of pressure/temptation to do what is immoral, unethical, unhealthy, or some unholy combination thereof. Sometimes our craving for approval or companionship, and our personal insecurity or lack of faith in God compel us to engage in bad behavior.

We might be better off severing some unhealthy relationships. We are not called to isolate ourselves from the world; we're actually called to go to the ends of the Earth to make disciples. But in certain instances we need to step back from a situation for our own spiritual health and growth.

Are our friends or coworkers bringing us down? We might need to pray about it and make a change.

Day 32

May 6

Psalm 89:1 "I will sing about the Lord's faithful love forever."

George Washington

No Party Affiliation

Worship

On this day in 1778, the American Army stationed at Valley Forge got some great news. The French had decided to join the Continentals' side during the Revolutionary War against the British, and word had trickled up to the Pennsylvania wilderness that had claimed so many lives the previous winter due to the cold weather, disease, and a severe food shortage.

George Washington and his men decided that nothing less than a celebration was in order. But before indulging in festivities, something more solemn took place: they had a worship service.

In an interesting contrast to the French Revolution, which occurred only a decade later and was characterized by a movement against religious authority and towards agnosticism, the Christian faith played a central role in the American Revolution. Washington insisted on Sunday services when feasible and sometimes performed the religious duties himself when a clergyman was not available.

These worship services were more than just an effort to follow tradition. May 6, 1778 was a Wednesday, but they held a worship service anyway because they were thankful for a development which they believed would mean the difference in winning the war.

What about us? How important is worship to us? Are we just going through the motions? Do we only think of worship as a Sunday morning activity? Do we go to the Lord when we get really good news, or do we only go to Him when we need something?

We need to be better than that today. We can worship just about any time, just about anywhere. And we should.

Day 33

May 7

James 1:19 "My dear brothers and sisters, understand this: Everyone should be quick to listen, slow to speak, and slow to anger."

Abraham Lincoln

Republican Party

Guarding our Tongues

On this day in the year 1837, Abraham Lincoln wrote one of his multiple letters to Mary Owens in an effort to discourage her from the idea of marrying him. If you are thinking, "Wait, Lincoln married Mary Todd," you are correct. But before Mary Todd was in the picture, Lincoln met Owens when she came to town to see her sister.

After Owens left, Lincoln said if she ever came back, he was going to marry her.

Unfortunately, he said this in front of the wrong person, because it got back to Owens, who decided it was a great idea. Upon further reflection though, Lincoln had misgivings. He communicated through multiple letters that if Owens returned and they got married, she would be unhappy and poor, and she really needed to think things through. After a while, she got the hint(s).

Lincoln had not officially proposed, but he had said too much. And so it is with us. We can be too incautious in our words. We speak up too soon, without all the facts, and with language that is too extreme. There are times when we would do well to meditate on the middle part of James' advice to us. There are times when we need to be "slow to speak."

Day 34

May 10

I Corinthians 4:16 "Therefore I urge you to imitate me."

Theodore Roosevelt

Republican Party

Lead by Example

This day in 1898 marked the last day Theodore Roosevelt was assistant secretary of the navy. He left his job to go fight in the Spanish-American War. One argument peace activists have made over the years is that wars are usually declared by old politicians, but it is young men (now young men and women) who will have to fight and die in them.

Roosevelt was different. He could have said he was doing his part to support the war effort by helping coordinate our naval forces, and this would have a bigger contribution to American success than anything he could do in uniform. And he would have been correct. But it didn't matter. Roosevelt wasn't going to let other people fight a war on his behalf.

The point here is not how an individual might feel about war policy; it's that actions speak louder than words. We can speak eloquently about what other people need to do, but we are better role models when we lead by example.

Day 35

May 11

Psalm 139:14 "I will praise You because I have been remarkably and wondrously made. Your works are wondrous, and I know this very well."

Grover Cleveland

Democratic Party

Self-Worth

On this day in 1894, The Pullman Strike started and impacted railroads all over the country. The issues were connected to a depression that hit the country the year before. The Depression of 1893 was the worst one in American history until the Great Depression struck in 1929.

Grover Cleveland was President at this point, and he enjoyed a rare distinction: He was one of only three Presidents to win the popular vote at least three times (Andrew Jackson and Franklin Roosevelt were the others). Cleveland was originally elected in 1884, won the popular vote but not the Electoral College in 1888, then retook the White House after the Election of 1892.

Cleveland was a conservative who believed the federal government should not overstep its strict constitutional bounds, and the majority of the voters were okay with that for three elections in a row. When the economy turned bad, however, many people called for more action. Cleveland resisted partially because he did not trust Congress to responsibly handle large sums of money or big programs.

Subsequently, the country turned against Cleveland and the Democrats in the next election. Cleveland was steadfast, but perceptions of him changed. Perceptions are fickle. We don't have to base our feelings of self-worth and confidence on the ebb and flow of what others think of us. We should derive our self-worth from our Creator. We can be confident of His work. We don't need to figure out our self-worth; we can put our confidence in the One who made us. He does the best work.

Day 36

May 16

Proverbs 13:6 "Righteousness guards people of integrity, but wickedness undermines the sinner."

Andrew Johnson

Democratic Party

Integrity

On this day in 1868, Andrew Johnson survived his impeachment process by one vote. When a President gets impeached, it simply means he goes on trial in the Senate. It takes a two-thirds majority vote in the Senate for the President to be kicked out of office. For those keeping score at home, two Presidents have been impeached but not convicted: Andrew Johnson and Bill Clinton. Richard Nixon would have experienced both, in the opinion of some of the senators from his own party, but he resigned from office before they could take his job away from him.

Andrew Johnson was on trial in the Senate because technically he broke the law, but mostly because he was pro-South after the North had won the Civil War, and John Wilkes Booth had murdered President Lincoln. In short, Johnson's politics were all wrong. And he was a jerk when it came to getting along with the rich and powerful.

Johnson survived in office because his detractors fell one vote short. The final vote came from Edmund Ross who didn't like Johnson personally, nor did the senator care for Johnson's politics. But Ross decided that what they were doing to Johnson was wrong. Ross figured he was committing political suicide by sparing Johnson, and Ross was right on both counts—Congress was in the wrong, and Ross never won another election. Doing the right thing can cost us something, and sometimes the cost is high. Ross wasn't a perfect man, we've only had One of those, but Ross was virtuous in this matter, even though it wasn't easy. That's integrity.

We need to be people of integrity today.

Day 37

May 25

Ecclesiastes 4:12 "And if someone overpowers one person, two can resist him. A cord of three strands is not easily broken."

James Madison

Democratic-Republican Party

Teamwork

On this day in 1787, the Constitutional Convention started. I mention this because I am going to talk about James Madison, who is often called "the Father of the Constitution." Madison is an interesting figure because he had an amazing capacity to work with different kinds of men and get really substantive things done.

Madison worked with his fellow Virginian and philosophical soulmate Thomas Jefferson to start one of our first political parties, the Democratic-Republicans (it's today's Democratic Party).

Madison was also a strong ally of George Washington through the Revolutionary War and well into Washington's first term as President, despite Washington's open disdain for political parties. Their alliance is also interesting because of their personal differences. Madison was a well-schooled and brilliant man of ideas, and he was small physically (about 5½ feet tall and a 100 pounds). Though intelligent, Washington lacked a formal education. Also, Washington was a man of action and a physical behemoth for his day (about 6 feet, 2 inches and 200 pounds).

Another study in contrasts with Madison was Ben Franklin. Madison was rich, a shy southerner, and a man who never left American soil. Franklin was born into a working-class family, a charming Yankee, and a frequent traveler to Europe. Franklin was also much older than Madison, but they worked well together politically.

No matter what our talents are, we can get more done if we work with others. If we are willing to work with people who are different than us, the sky's the limit.

Day 38

May 26

I John 4:7 "Dear Friends, let us love one another, because love is from God, and everyone who loves has been born of God and knows God."

George Washington

No Political Party Affiliation

Love

On this day in 1789, George Washington opened the home of the Chef Executive to the public. There was no White House yet, there wasn't even a Washington DC, but Washington established the precedent that the leader of the country would be accessible to the people. The United States would not have a government protected by palace guards; it would instead be a government of the people. Average everyday Americans could walk right up, knock on the President's door, and expect someone to answer it. Typically, it would not be Washington himself opening the door—he had people for that—but citizens could expect him to be available at certain times of the day.

Obviously, security is a little tighter in the 21st Century, but the idea that there should be a connection between the President and the people has been a part of the DNA of our government for over 200 years.

As Christians, we need to be accessible to people too. Some of us are better at following rules than we are at loving people. Some of us are content to love our fellow believers in our little Christian bubbles. We need to open our doors to people, either literally or metaphorically, and show them the love of Christ today. We need to pray for the strength to do that, even if it doesn't sound easy.

Day 39

May 28

John 13:34-35 "I give you a new command: Love one another. Just as I have loved you, you are also to love one another. By this everyone will know that you are my disciples. If you love one another."

Andrew Jackson

Democratic Party

Love one Another

On this day in 1830, Andrew Jackson signed the Indian Removal Act into law. It empowered the federal government to transport any Native American tribes east of the Mississippi to the Old West—by force if necessary.

In the frontier community where Jackson grew up, on the border of North and South Carolina, raids by the Native Americans were a terrifying reality. Rather than making distinctions among tribes, Jackson erred on the side of hostility and distrust towards all of them. Moving the tribes west made life safer for white Americans, according to Jackson. He wasn't totally wrong, but he also wasn't totally fair.

Surprisingly, Jackson adopted a Native American baby. The child was orphaned by an attack on his Creek village. Jackson was orphaned as a teenager, so his act of mercy makes sense. But Jackson lacked empathy for Native Americans before and after this, which makes it unusual.

People are complicated, but that's only kind of the point. When we've been hurt or burned, it can create hostility within us, and some people—Christians included—will become hostile to a whole group because of the actions of a handful of people. But we are called to love everybody, not just the nice, easy-to-figure-out people who are just like us. We have to love people even when they are mean, complicated, or weird.

My prayer as I worked on this book was that the Holy Spirit would direct me. The specific devotions are also driven by the dates of the events. I find it interesting that we have two devotions in a row dealing with love. Maybe that's because we all really need to work on this.

Day 40

May 28

Judges 6:15-16 "He (Gideon) said to him, 'Please, Lord, how can I deliver Israel? Look, my family is the weakest in Manasseh, and I am the youngest in my father's family.'

"'But I will be with you,' the Lord said to him. 'You will strike Midian down as if it were one man.'"

James Polk

Democratic Party

Dream Big

Something strange happened on this day in 1844. The delegates of the Democratic National Convention had gathered together a few days earlier for the purposes of electing a candidate for the presidency and agreeing on a party platform. Former President Martin Van Buren had the support of the majority of the delegates that year, despite being trounced in his reelection bid in 1840 by William Henry Harrison. Weirdly, though, having a majority was not enough. The delegates who didn't want another dose of Van Buren orchestrated things so that the standard bearer would need a two-thirds majority. As predicted, Van Buren fell short of that. Obviously, the other candidates for the title were even further off the mark. After a few days of wrangling, the shot-callers decided on a compromise candidate: James K. Polk of Tennessee. Polk had been interested in the proceedings at the DNC because he was hoping he might catch a little good fortune and be the choice for the VP position. He got much more than he bargained for and several months later was elected President.

Many of us are guilty of dreaming too small. In a world of great need, it is important for us to take bold steps of faith.

We need to dream big today.

Day 41

June 7

Proverbs 27:17 "Iron sharpens iron, and one person sharpens another."

Thomas Jefferson

Democratic-Republican Party

Accept Hard Feedback

In the United States, we celebrate our nation's birth on July 4 because this is when we declared our independence. The Declaration of Independence, written primarily by the future third President of the United States Thomas Jefferson, was an important document reflecting the will of the Continental Congress. As such, when the first draft of the document was presented to the members of Congress on June 7, 1776, they had a lot of feedback.

Jefferson got pretty upset with all the criticism from his supposed friends, and he was tempted to walk away from the project. Who were these people to question his insights? None of them were good enough to get asked to write it. Fortunately, Ben Franklin, smooth talking diplomat that he was, convinced Jefferson to try again, and things unfolded as they needed to.

Negative feedback can be brutal, but sometimes it is necessary. We aren't perfect; we fall short. Sometimes we can't see that, or pretend we don't. As we receive input on spiritual things, it can be tempting and easy to get defensive, as Jefferson did. But getting defensive doesn't make me a better ambassador of Christ. Sometimes people who criticize us are wrong. Are we strong enough, though, to listen to them when they're right? We need to be. Pray for the intestinal fortitude to learn from a good critiquing (or maybe even a bad one).

Day 42

June 8A

Psalm 19:1 "The heavens declare the glory of God, and the expanse proclaims the work of His hands."

Theodore Roosevelt

Republican Party

Respect God's Handiwork

On this day in 1906, Teddy Roosevelt signed the Antiquities Act into law. It was the first serious effort at the national level to protect the natural resources of the United States. This was not a politically-motivated move by the 26th President; Roosevelt was a genuine nature lover. He flirted with the idea of being a park ranger or a natural scientist. Coming from a wealthy family, though, he felt an obligation to either pursue something lucrative (so he wasn't a drain on the family fortune) or devote himself to public service. Obviously, he chose public service, but he never got over his love affair with nature.

It is easy for some of us to take nature for granted. Others among us, like Teddy Roosevelt, love the outdoors. Wherever one falls on the spectrum, we would do well to consider God's handiwork. The beauty and diversity of nature is a testament to a loving Creator God. We are created in God's image, so we should be characterized as people who build things/situations/people up, rather than tearing them down.

Consider how big and majestic the night sky is. Consider the beauty and diversity in nature. These things should give us a sense of humility before the Lord.

Let us pray that we will be humble builders today, rather than something less than that.

Day 43

June 8B

Proverbs 19:21 "Many plans are in a person's heart, but the Lord's decree will prevail."

James Madison

Democratic-Republican Party

Accepting Plan B

James Madison had a lot of good ideas. On this day in 1789, he presented 20 such ideas to the House of Representatives to be considered as amendments. These were whittled down to ten and formed the basis for the Bill of Rights.

This is just one example of how incredibly influential Madison was on the development of the United States. But he almost took a much different path. Years earlier, he joined the Virginia Militia. The life of a soldier wasn't the best fit for a 100-pound man on the south side of five and a half feet, especially when that man had a medical problem that historians think might have been epilepsy. Maybe in a time of peace, Madison could have carved out a niche in the military, but as the Americans were moving towards a war against the most powerful empire in the world, a soldier's life was not a good fit for him.

Madison pursued this path though, until he couldn't.

Madison's Plan B—a career in politics—led to a much greater impact on the American way of life. And so it is with us at times. We plan, we hope, we maneuver. Sometimes our plans come to fruition, and sometimes God wants us doing something different. Madison could have sat at home on his plantation, he could have felt sorry for himself, but instead he threw everything he had into his next opportunity.

As we have seen with James Madison and James Polk, sometimes God has something bigger for us when we are open to it.

Day 44

June 11

Matthew 18:15 "If your brother sins against you, go and rebuke him in private. If he listens to you, you have won your brother."

George Washington

No Party Affiliation

Conflict Resolution

On this day in 1777, George Washington forgave a man who betrayed him. In a surprise move, though, the act of forgiveness is not the point of today's devotional.

What happened was Washington's aide sent a letter to another American general accusing Washington of being indecisive, and thus incompetent to lead the Continental Army. The aide suggested he and the recipient of the letter, plus other leaders, should go to Congress and declare that Washington should get replaced.

The perception of Washington's alleged indecisiveness probably came from the Virginian's natural inclination towards bold action in war colliding with his recognition of the need for restraint and caution against an enemy with overwhelming advantages. But this isn't the point either.

When Washington discovered his aide's betrayal, the aide was humiliated. His insubordination could have ruined his career. Washington left the man wallowing in mortification for a little while but eventually forgave him.

Here's the point: When Washington finally chose to address the matter, he told his aide that the man was entitled to his opinion, but if he had concerns about Washington's leadership, then the aide should have addressed them with Washington directly. It is so much easier to complain about someone than it is for us to try and talk to them, but the model the Bible gives us is to try talking to the person first. Really, it's the Golden Rule in action. We would rather be talked to than talked about, so we should give others the same consideration. Some of us need to pray today for the intestinal fortitude to have a hard and awkward conversation that we've been putting off.

Day 45

June 12

Galatians 2:11 "But when Cephas (Simon Peter) came to Antioch, I opposed him to his face because he stood condemned."

Ronald Reagan

Republican Party

Confrontations

"Mr. Gorbachev, tear down this wall!" Ronald Reagan famously said on this day in 1987. The structure in question was the Berlin Wall, which held back East Berliners from the freedoms and opportunities found in West Berlin.

Supporters of the President appreciated his boldness. Critics thought it was unhelpful and needlessly confrontational. When Russian troops pulled out of East Germany two years later, the people of Berlin no longer cared what the Russian leader or Reagan's critics thought about it. The Germans tore down the wall themselves.

Reagan was on the right side of history on this matter. He wasn't afraid to speak bluntly on this issue. Some of us aren't always so bold. It is often tempting to avoid trouble, to delay an uncomfortable confrontation. But some issues only get worse when we won't deal with them.

Sometimes hard confrontations have to happen. If you need to have one, pray for grace. Pray also for boldness.

Day 46

June 14

I Samuel 17:33 "But Saul replied, 'You (David) can't go fight the Philistine. You're just a youth, and he's been a warrior since he was young.'"

Donald Trump

Republican Party

Exceeding Expectations

On this day in the year 1946, Donald Trump was born. To say his time in office has been controversial would be the kind of insight that ranks up there with water being wet and Siberia being cold in the wintertime.

Is President Trump "Making America Great Again," or is he the biggest threat to the American way of life as we know it? The answer you get will depend on who you ask.

Perhaps most of us can at least agree on this about the 45th President: He exceeded expectations just by getting elected. Many in the media were not only predicting a Hillary Clinton victory, they were saying it would be a landslide. Seriously. Do a YouTube search of "Predictions of Hillary Clinton Landslide" and check out your viewing options.

My point is not to disrespect the media; it's that even experts who study things can draw wrong conclusions. We would all consider ourselves experts on, um, ourselves, yet sometimes we don't think we're capable of being effective workers for God. This really says more about our faith in God than it does about our faith in ourselves. But besides that, sometimes we listen too well to the voices of others who don't believe in us. It's good to get input, but it is important for us to remember that God will see us through what He has called us to. When we are on God's side, we can exceed the expectations of others. We can even exceed the expectations of ourselves.

Day 47

July 2

Psalm 116:12 "How can I repay the Lord for all the good He has done me?"

James Garfield

Republican Party

Counting our Blessings

On this day in 1881, something sad happened. James Garfield was shot. Since x-ray machines and sterile medical procedures were unknown back then, a doctor stuck his non-sterilized finger into the bullet wound and wiggled it around to find the slug. When he was unable to feel the bullet, the next course of action was clear: Find a doctor with a longer finger. They did, but the result was the same.

With this type of medical care—the best in the country at the time—it is perhaps no shock that Garfield died. It took him almost three months to do so.

What's the moral of the story? Count your blessings. Because I am a historian, people occasionally ask me, if I could pick any time period to live in, when would it be? I always answer with some variation of, "I would only want to live in today's culture—we have modern medicine, air conditioning, and toothpaste."

There are limits to what doctors know, and there are other uncertainties in life, but we are surrounded by blessings. Let's count our blessings today, and thank God for them.

Day 48

July 4

Psalm 20:7 "Some take pride in chariots, and others in horses, but we take pride in the name of the Lord our God."

Calvin Coolidge

Republican Party

Trust in the Lord

Calvin Coolidge was a Yankee Doodle Dandy. John Adams, Thomas Jefferson, and James Monroe had all died on July 4, but Coolidge was the only President born on this special day. How perfect is that for a man who wants to evoke an image of himself closely associated with the country? Voting for Coolidge back then might have felt almost…patriotic.

Doesn't it seem like some people catch all the breaks? Does it ever feel like everybody else catches a break now and again except you? There have certainly been times when I felt that way.

When Saul was the popular choice of the Israelites to be king, and David was the youngest son in a big family and a run of the mill shepherd, who would have predicted how things would turn out?

When I attended college, I heard that some of the ladies had created an imaginary calendar of the guys who were the best catches. One of my friends was Mr. April. Another one was, I think, Mr. July. There were some days when I felt like I wouldn't have gotten in if it was a 365-day calendar.

We can focus on what we lack, we can focus on what other people have, and we can make ourselves miserable. Or, we can put our trust in the Lord and go do great things for His sake.

Day 49

July 9

Psalm 20:7 "Some take pride in chariots, and others in horses, but we take pride in the Name of the Lord our God."

Zachary Taylor

Whig Party

Trust in the Lord

On July 4, 1850, Zachary Taylor became violently ill. It had been a particularly hot Independence Day, and towards evening, the tired and sweaty President ate a large quantity of cherries and drank a lot of milk and water. Shortly thereafter, he became extremely sick, went downhill in a hurry, and died on July 9.

His demise was so quick and unexpected that some people suspected foul play. Rumors persisted to the point that in the 1990s, his remains were dug up and tested to see if the President was murdered. What kind of test can reveal poisoning 140+ years after the fact? For the answer to that, um, read a different book.

What is more relevant here is the irony of Taylor's situation. He was a hero in the Mexican War and beloved by his troops over the years for being willing to share in their hardships, which earned him the affectionate nickname "Old Rough and Ready." And yet, as tough as he was, he was done in by a bowl of fruit and maybe some bad milk.

No matter how strong we are, our bodies are fragile and temporary things. And so it is with all of our assets. This could be a scary thing, but it doesn't have to be: We can trust in the Lord.

Note: As stated before, I did not write these devotions in order. I wrote the July 9 entry and chose the Scripture months before I read through the manuscript and completed the July 4 entry. But we ended up with the same point and the same Scripture for two entries in a row. What is the Lord telling us?

Trust Him.

Day 50

July 11

Judges 16:28A "He called out to the Lord, 'Lord God, please remember me. Strengthen me, God, just once more.'"

William Howard Taft

Republican Party

Keep the Faith

On this day in 1921, William Howard Taft was sworn in as Chief Justice of the Supreme Court. Even by the standards of a presidential story, this is an amazing last act. Biographies of Presidents are fascinating because they are all so unlikely. Consider America today: There are over 300 million citizens alive right now, and only one is the President. It doesn't matter how rich, talented, or charismatic a person is, he or she has a better chance of winning the lottery twice than being elected to the presidency once. Thus, every story of someone becoming President is a tale of a unique and special journey.

Even by these standards, Taft has a great story.

He rode the coattails of the transcendently popular Theodore Roosevelt and got elected to the White House. Taft then proceeded to become one of the least likable Presidents ever. He wasn't a jerk, he just bothered people for a variety of reasons that can't adequately be covered in one page here.

Taft was so unpopular in fact that he finished in THIRD place when he was up for reelection!

But his story wasn't over. Warren Harding picked Taft to be the Chief Justice of the Supreme Court, making Taft the only person to hold this position and the presidency. It was easy to imagine that Taft's career in public service was over after the presidency, but we aren't nearly as good at predicting the future as we think we are.

As long as we are breathing, God can still use us. Instead of being chained to yesterday's failures, let's choose to have faith that God can use us today. The Lord might just have something amazing in store. We can choose to believe that, regardless of what yesterday looked like.

Day 51

July 17

I Peter 2:12 "Conduct yourselves honorably among the Gentiles, so that when they slander you as evildoers, they will observe your good works and will glorify God on the day He visits."

George Washington, John Adams, Thomas Jefferson

No Party Affiliation, Federalist, Democratic-Republican

Do Right

When James Callender died on this day in 1803, few Americans mourned. Callender was a newspaper journalist who would have been quite at home in our modern world of polarized cable news, angry social media rants, and hot takes. He skewered George Washington in the press, even as the majority of the country held the old general up on a pedestal. Callendar basically committed libel against John Adams, who was overbearing and sometimes insufferable, but not an adulterer or a pervert, as Callender alleged. Callender ruined the career, which included presidential aspirations, of Alexander Hamilton by exposing an affair between the married Hamilton and a married woman.

Mostly, though, Callender is remembered for exposing the story of Thomas Jefferson fathering several children by a slave named Sally Hemings.

There are two thoughts to ponder today. One, there are powerful men who use that power to their advantage when it comes to women. If you are a man in power, resist that temptation. If you are a woman in that situation, resist that pressure. Sally Hemings was a slave without options back then; today there are options. Two, if we are in a position of power, male or female, there are people who will criticize us. Sometimes fairly, because—let's face it—we're not perfect, but sometimes unfairly. If we are going to lead, we are going to catch some heat. If we try extra hard to please everybody, we'll catch heat for that, too. We can strive to do our best, so when the criticism comes, it might be recognized as being unwarranted. Of course, it is impossible for us to be perfect, but we can pray for wisdom and strength to know and do what is right.

Day 52

July 24

I Corinthians 11:1 "Imitate me, as I also imitate Christ."

Bill Clinton

Democratic Party

John Kennedy

Democratic Party

Be a Role Model

When Bill Clinton was 16, he and a bunch of other school kids from Arkansas had the opportunity to visit John Kennedy, the President of the United States. When Clinton actually got the chance to shake hands with the leader of the free world, as US Presidents were sometimes called back then, it was an electrifying moment for young Clinton. He decided in that moment that he wanted to grow up and become President.

People are watching us. Perhaps they aren't watching us with the awe of a young Democrat meeting his hero for the first time, but people are watching us even when we don't realize it.

What kind of role models are we? It might be tempting to object to the question, but we don't really have that luxury. Jesus Christ died on the cross for our sins. He conquered death because He loves us. We are new creations if we have been born again in Christ. We are parts of a royal priesthood; we are ambassadors for Christ. The only question is whether or not we are good ambassadors.

"Oh no," you might say, "I'm not fit to be a Christian role model."

I agree. Neither am I. But I believe the Holy Spirit is powerful enough to do His work through me (and I'm not even a Pentecostal).

I believe the Holy Spirit can work through you, too.

We need to go out with God's help and be Christian role models today.

Day 53

July 27

Philippians 4:7 "And the peace of God, which surpasses all understanding, will guard your hearts and minds in Christ Jesus."

Dwight Eisenhower

Republican Party

Peace

On this day in 1953 an armistice was signed ending the fighting in the Korean War. Dwight Eisenhower was able to negotiate only a cessation of warfare, not a full-fledged peace treaty. North and South Korea were not able to resolve their differences, chief among them: their styles of government. North Korea stayed Communist; South Korea maintained its democracy. The Koran peninsula has not known a true peace in all the years since. I am not blaming Dwight Eisenhower for this. The original United Nations' plan was to save South Korea from being swallowed up by North Korea, and that was a success.

Still, though, an armistice—a temporary cease fire—is not the same as securing a lasting peace.

In the same way, we often settle for temporary and imperfect solutions in turbulent and stressful times in our lives instead of turning to the Prince of Peace. We try to fix our circumstances instead of affixing our gaze on Christ first, and then trusting Him to guide us through our circumstances. We are promised a peace "which surpasses all understanding." My logic and strategizing cannot provide that. Neither can yours. Let us pray for peace from the Prince of Peace today.

Day 54

July 28

Isaiah 6:8 "Then I heard the voice of the Lord, asking, 'Who should I send? Who will go for us?' I said, 'Here I am. Send me.'"

George Washington

No Party Affiliation

New Opportunities

Did you know that July 28 is National Dance Day, or that there even was such a thing as National Dance Day? I didn't either until I looked it up.

Here's something else you might not have known: George Washington was an amazing dancer. Seriously. He wasn't just a good dancer, he was extraordinary. Washington was a natural athlete who typically excelled at physical things.

There are people around us who have talents we don't know about. Even more interestingly, you probably have untapped gifts yourself. You could possess abilities you are not aware of because you have never been called upon to use them. Not abilities like super speed (though that would be awesome), but maybe technical abilities, or communication skills, or the capacity to keep your head in a crisis.

Sometimes the thing we see as a problem or crisis is actually a gift: It might be an opportunity to learn something important about ourselves.

A prayer for us to pray today could be that God would give us a different kind of opportunity to serve—an opportunity to be challenged and to spread our wings. Dynamic growth can happen when circumstances change.

Day 55

July 31

Matthew 7:5 "Hypocrite! First take the beam of wood out of your eye, and then you will see clearly to take the splinter out of your brother's eye."

Ulysses Grant

Republican Party

Sin

On this day in 1854, Ulysses Grant left the Army. This might sound wrong to you, if you remember the Civil War was fought in the 1860s.

Grant actually joined the Army a few decades before the Civil War and fought with distinction during the Mexican War of 1845-1848. But Grant had a problem. In 1854, he was in charge of payroll for his base, and a significant sum went missing. No one in authority seriously considered the possibility that Grant might have stolen the money, because there was a much more likely explanation: He was such a drunk that someone was able to steal it out from under his nose without him realizing what happened.

Accusations of alcoholism plagued Grant for many years to come.

It's easy to shake our heads at the failures of others when visible consequences result from poor behavior. However, the fact of the matter is that we all struggle with sin. Sometimes the consequences are not so obvious, and maybe the sins of some of us are easier to hide, but we all struggle. Maybe the person whose weakness isn't alcohol is addicted to gambling, porn, food, gossip, worry, lying, self-absorption, pain-relievers, or laziness. Maybe he or she is guilty of excuse-making instead of witnessing.

Rather than just shaking our heads at the imperfections of others, we need to get our own houses in order, which is impossible without the power of the Holy Spirit. We need to pray for others to be strong in the face of temptation, and we need to pray for holiness in our own lives.

Day 56

August 2

Ephesians 5:15-16 "Pay careful attention, then, to how you live—not as unwise people but as wise—making the most of the time, because the days are evil."

Warren Harding

Republican Party

Redeem the Time

On this day in 1923, President Warren Harding died suddenly. It was probably a heart attack. I say "probably" because his wife refused to allow an autopsy to be performed. One of his doctors wanted the autopsy because he was concerned the public and press might blame the President's death on negligent medical care.

The doctor's concerns are probably not important unless you're really interested in medicine…or the idea of the press jumping to conclusions…or criminally negligent homicide.

The lack of an autopsy is probably not fishy, unless you believe Mrs. Harding was upset with her husband because of his alleged affairs.

Why do I keep mentioning interesting tangents before dismissing them as unimportant?

Why have I overused the word "probably" in today's devotions?

For a lot of people, life is shorter than they think it is going to be, as Warren Harding discovered on August 2, 1923. Our culture today fears death. Often times, even among us church folk, there is a reluctance to face it. We thus lose the sense of urgency to do God's work. We don't say "No," we say, "Not now—not yet." We allow ourselves to be distracted by things like mildly interesting stories (including conspiracy theories).

Warren Harding was already thinking about his re-election campaign, but he died before that season arrived.

We are not guaranteed tomorrow. We are not guaranteed all of today. We need to redeem what time we have. We need to pray that the Lord will give us a vision for His work in our lives today.

Day 57

August 8

Romans 3:23 "For all have sinned and fall short of the glory of God."

Richard Nixon

Republican Party

Pride

This was Richard Nixon's last full day as president in the year 1974. He resigned, effective August 9, because of the Watergate Scandal.

News flash: If you are trying to obstruct justice by paying off witnesses and sabotaging tape recordings, and if you are doing this to undermine the American democratic system, it's a bad thing, especially when you're the President.

A sad aspect of the story of Richard Nixon is that he never publicly acknowledged the wrong he did. Even as he resigned, he simply said it was because of all of the controversy. He said he could no longer help govern the nation, so he was stepping aside. He tried to make his departure sound noble, even though he was simply quitting to avoid getting thrown out of office by Congress. The impeachment process had begun, and senators from Nixon's own party told him he did not have the votes to hold onto his job.

Even years later, the only "mistake" Nixon acknowledged was that he "gave them (his political adversaries) the sword," as he put it. In other words, his actions gave his enemies the leverage to get him out of office. But he never admitted to wrongdoing, even though many of his aides went to prison.

Sometimes our pride gets in the way of us acknowledging our shortcomings. But we can't fix what we won't admit. Acknowledging our sins is an important step towards asking forgiveness and turning away from them.

Day 58

August 9

Colossians 3:12 "Therefore, as God's chosen ones, holy and dearly loved, put on compassion, kindness, humility, gentleness, and patience."

Gerald Ford

Republican Party

Humility

Gerald Ford became President of the United States on this day in 1974. His presidency gives us a nice piece of presidential trivia: Ford is the only president who never won a national election. He was appointed to the vice presidency when Spiro Agnew resigned, and Ford took over the White House when Richard Nixon walked away from it.

More interestingly about Ford, he gave us one of the greatest presidential quotations ever. He didn't try to oversell his greatness. He wanted to communicate that he was just an average American, not some larger than life, semi-mythical hero. As he put it, "I'm a Ford, not a Lincoln."

This kind of attitude was also on display when he stated his preference that bands should play his college fight song when he entered the room, rather than the customary "Hail to the Chief."

He was a humble President, which is kind of an oxymoron. A person would have to think pretty highly of himself/herself to believe that he/she was the absolute most qualified person in America to become the Chief Executive. But again, Ford didn't originally run for President or the VP position.

All of that said, there's a phrase that should be a bigger oxymoron than "humble President:" Arrogant Christian. We are called to a life of humility and service. Servant leadership is a powerful witness. If any among us thinks we can get a little arrogant at times, we need to repent. Christ came to serve, and we are called to be like Him. Arrogance kills our witness. If any of us struggle with this, we must pray for mercy and a new attitude.

Day 59

August 12

Matthew 17:20B "For I truly tell you, if you have faith the size of a mustard seed, you will tell this mountain, 'Move from here to there,' and it will move. Nothing will be impossible for you."

Calvin Coolidge

Republican Party

Faith

On this day in 1877, Thomas Edison was credited with creating the first model of a phonograph. This was not relevant to anything presidential until the Election of 1924, when Calvin Coolidge became the first to record a campaign message on a phonograph record, so listeners could, um, listen. Coolidge and his team hoped to reach voters directly and inspire them with their very own message from the President. Coolidge had taken over for the deceased Warren Harding the year before and now hoped to be elected to serve four more years.

What makes this interesting, and not just a piece of trivia, is the man recording his voice for people to listen to over and over again was famously tightlipped. A popular story about Coolidge, probably apocryphal,* was that a woman sat next to him at a fancy DC dinner party and said, "I have bet someone a substantial amount of money that I can get you to say at least three words tonight."

The President replied, "You lose."

Coolidge typically had little to say, but he took advantage of a new, speech-based medium to help his cause. Likewise, we can step outside of what is comfortable for us to do what needs to be done today. In fact, it is especially when we move beyond our comfort zones that our faith grows. We are told our faith can move mountains; we should pray for the boldness to at least move ourselves outside our comfort zones.

*"Apocryphal" means something that is not true, but is nevertheless totally believable, like if I said I never dated in high school.

Day 60

August 18

Matthew 5:37 "But let your 'yes' mean 'yes,' and your 'no' mean 'no.' Anything more than this is from the evil one."

George H.W. Bush

Republican Party

Consistency

On this day in 1988, George H.W. Bush spoke at the Republican National Convention and uttered the words, "Read my lips: No new Taxes."

He actually, fatefully, said more than this. He talked about how the Democrat-controlled Congress was going to want to raise taxes, and he would say no, and they would come at him again and he would say no, etc., etc., until he would finally end the discussion by uttering his famous line. But in the end, they did not have to read his lips. George H.W. Bush broke his promise to Republicans and agreed to the biggest tax increase in American history.

He lost the love of many conservatives that day, but he didn't gain any real affection from liberals.

The point of this is not to debate tax policy; it is to say that sometimes we got caught up in the moment and zig when we had planned to zag. Either Bush wasn't sincere in his pledge, but wanted to please Republicans, or he truly believed in his tax policy of not raising taxes, but he wanted to appease a spirited opposition party and its allies in the media. Or Bush was sincere in his pledge, but then changed his mind. This does not cast him in a more favorable light though. He was a career politician running for President; he needed to understand the issue well enough after so many years to maintain a consistent policy, whichever side of the issue he was on.

For many Republicans, it wasn't just that Bush agreed to raise taxes; it was that he broke his promise and raised taxes.

As a believer, you need to be a person whose word is your bond. If we want people to believe what we say about Christ, it would help if people know we are trustworthy and consistent.

Day 61

August 20

Psalm 139:14 "I will praise you because I have been remarkably and wondrously made."

Benjamin Harrison

Republican Party

Self-Worth

Benjamin Harrison, born on this day in 1833, was the 23rd President of the United States. His grandfather, William Henry Harrison was the 9th President. I used to wonder if Benjamin's dad was alive when Benjamin got elected, and then I wondered if the dad felt like he didn't really measure up. If a man has a son who is President, and a dad who was a President, wouldn't it be easy for the man to think he had let the family down as he looked around the table at Thanksgiving dinner?

As it turns out, Benjamin Harrison's dad, John Scott Harrison, was a member of the House of Representatives who passed away before the 23rd President was elected. Thus, John Harrison probably did not struggle too much with feelings of having not measured up.

But what about us? Have we frustrated ourselves by making comparisons to other people? Do we feel like failures because we don't have the gifts and accomplishments of somebody else?

If God wanted one more of somebody else, he would have made them a twin. If that person already has a twin, um, never mind—we're getting off track.

The point is we need to focus on being the best version of who God has called us to be. We can certainly learn from other people, but we need to not measure our self-worth against anybody else.

Day 62

August 24

Deuteronomy 31:6 "Be strong and courageous; don't be afraid or terrified of them. For the Lord your God is the One who will go with you; He will not leave you or abandon you."

James Madison

Democratic-Republican Party

Don't Give Up

On this day in the year 1814, things looked bleak indeed for James Madison. The United States had been at war for two years, and dreams of snatching Canada away from the British had gone up in smoke sometime earlier. But at this point in August 1814, things had decidedly gone from bad to worse.

British forces had invaded Washington DC, and there was no stopping them. Madison stayed behind longer than most members of Congress, but continuing to stick around at this point would only end in him becoming a prisoner or a corpse. He fled to Virginia. The British celebrated by burning the White House and several other buildings in DC.

Madison, physically, was the smallest President in American history. In the years leading up to the Revolution, he had tried out for the Virginia militia, but he had health issues that precluded him from serving his country this way. And, now, added to the list of things he could not do was protect his White House. When the strongest country in the world (Britain) took over the capital, what hope did the Americans have?

A reasonable person might conclude that the Americans were out of options, and James Madison was a reasonable person. But he wasn't a quitter. The US continued to press on, and while it did not win the War of 1812, it did fight Britain to a stalemate. Madison ended up in a better situation than he otherwise would have because he did not quit.

What spiritual battles with sin are we privately involved in today? Do things look bleak? Does victory seem unlikely? Don't quit fighting.

Day 63

August 25

Matthew 10:16 "Look, I'm sending you out like sheep among wolves. Therefore, be as shrewd as serpents and as innocent as doves."

William McKinley

Republican Party

Wisdom

This was kind of a significant day in 1939: It was when the movie *The Wizard of Oz* opened. This might not seem that relevant to President William McKinley, who died in 1901, but it was. Before it was a movie, *The Wizard of Oz* was a novel by L. Frank Baum, and it was about McKinley.

More than one writer has pointed out the intentional parallels between the Election of 1900 and the characters of the book. Baum favored McKinley's opponent, William Jennings Bryan. Thus, the Wizard himself was a representation of McKinley, a powerful person in a faraway city who told people what they wanted to hear, but in the end helped no one but himself. The Cowardly Lion had a ferocious roar, but was nevertheless too timid for his own good, much like Jennings, who was a brilliant public speaker, but needed to be more aggressive in Baum's opinion. Dorothy (the poor, shoeless farm girl), the brainless Scarecrow (the uneducated rural man), and the Tinman (the factory worker toiling away in joyless, soulless misery) would form a coalition with the Cowardly Lion (Jennings), and they would march to the capital where all their dreams would come true (Bryan would win the election).

What's the obvious takeaway? L. Frank Baum was not a prophet.

Okay, but besides that, the point is that sometimes there is more to the story than meets the eye. We believers need to be shrewd in our dealings with the world. We don't need to be hostile and guarded, but we need to be smart when it comes to interpreting what's going on in the world around us. We should pray for wisdom today.

Day 64

September 6

Romans 12:12 "Rejoice in hope; be patient in affliction; be persistent in prayer."

William McKinley

Republican Party

Stress

This was a sad day in American history in the year 1901. William McKinley was shot during his second term as President. After the attack, one of the first things he said dealt with his wife. "Be careful how you tell her. Oh, be careful," he urged his team. Then he spoke to his security detail, which was in the process of pulverizing the shooter. "Be easy with him, boys."

If someone had just shot me twice at pointblank range, I don't know if I would have the character to be concerned about how he was doing. I think I might be preoccupied with my own issues at that point, like coping with the pain or not bleeding to death. But McKinley, who would eventually die of his wounds, was a better man than that. He wasn't focused on himself. Even in a time of calamity.

When we face stress today, where will our focus be? Will we be self-absorbed? Will we lash out at those around us? Will we lose our ability to sympathize with others? If we make the Lord our priority, He can give us the strength to focus on others during our moment of truth.

Day 65

September 11

Psalm 30:5 "For His anger lasts only a moment, but His favor, a lifetime. Weeping may stay overnight, but there is joy in the morning."

George W. Bush

Republican Party

Hope

This day in 2001 was pretty anxiety-ridden for many Americans. Three planes flew into buildings, and another one went down in a field. Thousands died. In some places, gas prices spiked. Sporting events began to get cancelled, not only because it was a somber time, but because people were apprehensive about getting together in large public groups when terrorists had just shown a willingness to do anything to attack such groups.

On that day I couldn't help but ask, "What's going to happen on September 12?" What was coming next? How could the United States beat an enemy that engaged in suicide missions? It's one thing to risk dying for a cause; it's another to know death is coming but carrying out the mission anyway.

George W. Bush faced a huge challenge. At first, the nation rallied around him, and his approval rating shot skyward. Eventually though, as the war in Iraq lingered and the economy contracted, Bush's popularity took a hit.

One reason for hope on 9/11 was remembering that the US had already defeated any enemy that engaged in suicide attacks: Japan in World War Two.

Another reason for hope is the truth found in today's Scripture. We are all acquainted with difficult, even crushing, times. But for those of us who are in Christ, we know that suffering might last for a season, but ultimately things will get better—maybe not in this life, but certainly in Heaven.

No matter how bad things are, if we have Christ in our hearts, we are guaranteed a happy ending. Take comfort in that truth today.

Day 66

September 19

Deuteronomy 34:7 'Moses was one hundred twenty years old when he died; his eyes were weak, and his vitality had not left him.'"

George Washington

No Party Affiliation

Managing Transitions

On this day in 1796, George Washington published his Farewell Address in the newspaper, announcing he would not serve a third time as President.

Washington was great, he was incomparable, but he was not immortal. He was old, and it was time to retire. Even the best of us don't stay on the job forever. We all need to call it quits at some point.

Many people quit too soon; some hold on too long. There are those, like Washington, who know they can hang on a little longer, but they believe it's time to turn the reigns over to someone else. We need to be careful to not be so vain, or so in need of validation, or so lacking in trust in God, that we don't know when to say when.

Part of Washington's greatness was that he knew when to walk away from power. He was not so addicted to it that he held onto it all the way to the grave.

The message here is not that we should be quitters; but, perhaps paradoxically, we do need to know when to quit. God gave us Moses, but He also gave us Joshua. Find your Joshua and start preparing him to see greater things than you. (I mean, help your protégé see greater things than you have seen. I'm not implying you're not great. You're reading my book, so why would I insult you?)

Day 67

September 20

Luke 9:23 "Then He said to them all, 'If anyone wants to follow after Me, let him deny himself, take up his cross daily, and follow me."

Chester Arthur

Republican Party

Exceeding Expectations

This was the first full day of the Chester Arthur Administration following the death of James Garfield in 1881. Arthur exceeded expectations, given that he was part of a political machine. A political machine was the name given to an organization run by a party boss. These bosses usually were members of ethnic or religious minorities who could not overcome the prejudices of the day and win political offices themselves. But they could influence elections enough to swing them for other people.

These party bosses would use the promise of jobs and other means to persuade enough voters to support a certain guy and get someone like Chester Arthur into office, then continue to help as Arthur and others climbed the political ladder. Typically, such politicians would use their influence in office to support the businesses of the party bosses, who would use that money not to just get richer, but to swing the next election.

One could appreciate the elegant simplicity of the system, if one did not get too fussy over the subversion of the democratic process.

Anyway, what is so surprising about Chester Arthur is that even though he was the product of such a corrupt system, when he became President, he turned into an honorable man (which certainly frustrated the party bosses).

If Chester Arthur can grow and change, we can, too, especially with the power of the Holy Spirit. Change is difficult, which is why Christ encourages us to take up our Cross daily. We can do better today than we did yesterday. Let's pray and strive for that.

Day 68

October 2

Galatians 6:5 "For each person will have to carry his own load."

Harry Truman

Democratic Party

Responsibility

On this day in 1945, Harry Truman received an engraving of a quotation that caught his eye. It read, "The buck stops here." When most people read or hear this, they assume Truman was accepting the responsibility for anything that happened in his administration. Actually, according to some sources, he simply meant the person in charge had to make the big decisions.

Either way, many of us struggle to live up to this motto. When we are unhappy, unsuccessful, or ungodly, we are often tempted to pass the buck. But we need to own our decisions and our baggage. We won't experience the growth we need to, we won't learn from our mistakes, and we won't truly repent of our sins, unless we take responsibility for what is going on in our lives.

A wise man once said something like "Success has a hundred fathers, but failure is an orphan." We sometimes don't want to accept our failures, but we often learn more from our failures than our successes. Among other things, we learn humility.

Where does our buck stop? Where will it stop today?

Day 69

October 11

Colossians 3:9 "Do not lie to one another, since you have put off the old self with its practices."

Jimmy Carter

Democratic Party

Honesty

On this day in 2002, Jimmy Carter won a Nobel Peace Prize, but he entered the world stage several years earlier by winning the Presidential Election of 1976.

It was not easy for an obscure governor from a small state (Georgia) to get elected to the presidency, but Carter came up with a lengthy game plan, and he followed it to victory. One of the items on his list was to develop a Kennedyesque smile. It wasn't a profound thing, but it was interesting, don't you think?

More relevant to his election was his promise, repeated over and over again, that he would not lie to the American people. Many said this was a naïve (at best) or insincere (at worst—but at least ironic) promise. But for a nation fed up with Lyndon Johnson's lies over Vietnam and Richard Nixon's lies over Watergate and Vietnam, a candidate committed to honesty sounded pretty good.

While few people are truly objective when it comes to politics, going by the numbers indicates that Carter was not popular or very successful. After four years in office, Carter only carried six states against Ronald Reagan in 1980. Ouch. But Carter did succeed in setting an example of integrity in the White House. His perceived failures dealt with the economy and foreign affairs, not honesty.

It's not easy to be an honest politician. Most of us aren't in government work, but we face our own ethical challenges. If we are not people of integrity, our Christian witness will be undermined, and we will have to answer for that before the One who knows all truth. We need to be people of integrity today.

Day 70

October 19

Colossians 4:2 "Devote yourselves to prayer; stay alert in it with thanksgiving."

George Washington

No Party Affiliation

Prayer

On this day in 1781, the Siege of Yorktown ended with the British Army surrendering to George Washington. The peace treaty would not be agreed upon until two years later, but this campaign pretty much ended the Revolutionary War. Who would have thought that the most powerful, disciplined army in the world could lose to the Americans? These "Colonials," as the British called them, had thirteen virtually independent states and a weak congress. Some Americans in the government were almost as afraid of a powerful American army as they were of the Redcoats. Some of the states were more interested in protecting their own interests than in focusing on supporting the Continental Army.

Despite having the deck stacked against him, Washington prevailed. The tall Virginian wasn't perfect, but he was, according to those who knew him, a praying man.

What about today? Do the obstacles seem too great? Or, are we, like the Redcoats of old, thinking *Today will be a piece of cake, I've got plenty of chariots and horses*? Um, metaphorically speaking.

Either way, we better pray today. We need to pray like we mean it.

Day 71

October 24

James 1:22 "But be doers of the Word and not hearers only, deceiving yourselves."

Herbert Hoover

Republican Party

Franklin Roosevelt

Democratic Party

Doers of the Word

This day in 1929 was known as "Black Thursday," and it is considered the start of the Great Depression. Herbert Hoover was on duty that year, and he became known as a do-nothing President, because, well, he didn't seem to do much.

This characterization isn't really accurate. As a political conservative, Hoover's inclination was to not have a government meddling in people's affairs, but when he saw that this economic downturn was worse than anything Americans had ever experienced, he actually tried to do several things. But Hoover's efforts did not make much of a difference, and certainly in comparison to Franklin Roosevelt's New Deal, Hoover's moves amounted to small potatoes.

How are we perceived as Christians? Maybe we do a lot of things for the Kingdom of God, and people see that. Maybe, like Hoover we try to do things, but people don't see their impact. For many of us, our faith is demonstrated more by the bad stuff we don't do, rather than the good stuff we were called to do. We all have reasons for what we don't get done. A lot of times we also have excuses. Are we doing the Lord's work every day, or do we mostly just show up on Sunday morning and watch other people work?

What are we doing to share the Gospel with people who are spiritually dying without it? Today, let's dedicate ourselves to doing something to communicate God's love to people who desperately need to hear about it.

Day 72

October 27

Luke 6:40 "A disciple is not above his teacher, but everyone who is fully trained will be like his teacher."

Theodore Roosevelt

Republican Party

Discipleship

This day was Teddy Roosevelt's birthday in 1858. When he was a kid, his dad told him he had a first-rate mind, but his body was weak. Young Roosevelt, who idolized his father, spent the rest of his life trying to prove he was strong enough to handle whatever life threw at him. He pretty much succeeded.

This is a great aspect of the success story of Theodore Roosevelt. There is a genuine satisfaction in working out and being able to do something physically that we were unable to do before, and there is also a feeling of accomplishment when we only succeed after demonstrating a lot of grit.

All of that said, there is a type of training that is more valuable than physical workouts or mental toughness. There are spiritual disciplines that have been practiced for thousands of years: praying, fasting, meditating on Scripture, and others. Many Christians want the benefits of faith, but aren't dedicated to the discipline side of being a disciple; just as many people want to lose weight and gain energy and strength, but they aren't serious about eating right and exercising. Or, they want to accomplish something big without having to persevere for it.

Roosevelt lived the rough and tumble life of a cowboy for a few years and later boxed, learned a martial art, power walked, went on safaris, and read a book a day. These were all things that did not seem likely when he was a sickly little kid. Just because we have been weak in our discipleship before now, it doesn't mean we need to stay that way. We need to prayerfully consider (then implement) a plan for discipleship.

Day 73

October 30

Romans 12:18 "If possible, as far as it depends on you, live at peace with everyone."

John Adams

Federalist Party

Getting Along

On this day in 1735, John Adams was born. He was a brilliant man and a better orator than his friends, George Washington and Thomas Jefferson. Speaking of whom, it was kind of impressive that Adams, who tended to irritate people, was somehow able to be friends with both Washington and Jefferson, even though they did not like each other.

Nevertheless, Adams had a flaw, and it contributed greatly to his aforementioned tendency to get on people's nerves. Adams had a lot of ambition. What is especially interesting about this is that he recognized his ambition as a potential character flaw, and he committed himself to a course of action to keep it under control. He wanted to be recorded in history books, and he wanted history to be kind to him. He was afraid that his ambition to be in power and influence national affairs might compel him to compromise his values, so he tried to keep his ambition in check by sometimes arguing for measures he knew were unpopular and doomed to failure (thus he could prove to himself and others that he was not a slave to popularity).

So, John Adams was a noble person, which is great, but what could be more irritating than a guy who argues for unpopular things on purpose just to prove how virtuous he is?

There really is something to be said for living "at peace with everyone." Some of us like to argue, some of us are contrary, but we need to acknowledge that Jesus taught "blessed are the peacemakers."

Day 74

November 2A

Proverbs 18:24 "A man that hath friends must shew himself friendly, and there is a Friend that sticketh closer than a brother." KJV

Andrew Jackson

Democratic Party

Support System

Andrew Jackson became an orphan when his mother died on November 2, 1781. He was 14. The 7th President's father and brother had passed away earlier. Death was a frequent companion for many people back then, but this was a lot for a boy to bear.

Jackson grew up and became remarkably successful as a war hero, a politician, and eventually as the first two-term President from outside the state of Virginia.

These successes don't paint the whole picture with Jackson, though. He could be remarkably thin-skinned and passionately angry. His infamous duels and tirades were not the result of happenstance. Jackson could be loving and loyal, but he was a hothead. He was driven by insecurities that resulted not just from the sinful nature we all have, but also by the lack of the support of a stable family unit at such a young age.

We have no control over the home we grew up in, but as believers we have a family today—the Family of God. The Church is a Body. One of the ways God chooses to show His love to us is through the people in His Church. If you are thinking, "My church isn't that loving," well, we can't control other people either. But we can choose to be part of a loving support system for other believers. God chose to wire into us a need to be loved and a need to love. We are not supposed to be alone on this journey through life. We are carrying burdens that are easier to bear when we are in fellowship with others. We need to be a friend to someone today.

Day 75

November 2B

II Corinthians 2:17 "Therefore, if anyone is in Christ, he is a new creation; the old has passed away, and see, the new has come!"

James Polk

Democratic Party

Self-Worth

This day in 1795 was James K. Polk's birthday. Don't be embarrassed if you didn't get him something. To be fair, he didn't get you anything either.

Polk has always been an interesting President because opinions on him vary so widely. We are used to this with modern Presidents. Conservatives and moderates have a high opinion of Ronald Reagan; liberals tend to hate him. Liberals and moderates love John Kennedy; some conservatives think he's vastly overrated. But with earlier Presidents, usually our opinions are more consistent. Almost everybody loves Abraham Lincoln, and they have virtually nothing good to say about James Buchanan, but with both men, there is a consistency of opinion.

When it comes to Polk, though, perceptions are divided. Critics say he stirred up the slavery issue, then walked away from the presidency. People who like him say he had a clear agenda, he accomplished as much as he could, then he was willing to go home. He only served one term because that was what he promised, then he left office in a statesman-like fashion. He wasn't desperate for power and relevance.

People's opinions of him vary, but that does not change who he was. In our own lives, people will judge us good and bad. Some will think we are better than we see ourselves. Some people will not give us credit for our positives. Different perceptions of us do not change who we are. As believers, we are children of God and new creations in Christ. That sounds pretty special.

Day 76

November 4

Proverbs 31:25 "Strength and honor are her clothing, and she can laugh at the time to come."

Abraham Lincoln

Republican Party

Faith and Humor

Abraham Lincoln was smitten on this day in 1842. He was at a dance, and there was Mary Todd—the apple of his eye. Lincoln tried to woo her with a combination of boldness and honesty—not a bad strategy in many of life's situations.

He walked up to her and said something like, "I want to dance with you in the worst way."

She later remarked with a grin, "He did."

The humor of Mary Todd Lincoln was not as widely displayed as her husband's, but it wasn't bad.

Mr. Lincoln used humor to cope with the stress and tragedy in his life. His mother died when he was young, his father basically abandoned him and his sister temporarily to go get another wife, Lincoln's beloved sister died several years later, and so did his first love. Several of his children died young, and he was the President during the most divisive and bloodiest war in American history.

Another way he handled the pressure was he started thinking and talking about God a lot. Was the increasingly religious talk just calculated rhetoric from a shrewd politician? This might have been partially the case, yet Lincoln would hardly be unique for turning to the Lord when faced with overwhelming stress and the loss of loved ones (as well as the loss of hundreds of thousands of troops under his authority).

Humor and faith can get us through a lot of things. Positive humor can create a light and happy tone. Faith can move mountains. We should pray for both as we face the day.

Day 77

November 5

Proverbs 22:13 "The Sluggard says there's a lion in the streets."

Abraham Lincoln

Republican Party

Excuses

On this date in 1862, Abraham Lincoln fired General George McClellan, commander of the Union's Army of the Potomac. McClellan had a lot of strengths—he was a sharp dresser, he looked comfortable on a horse (which was a bigger deal when generals spent a lot of time on horseback), and he was legitimately good at training troops. He also excelled at making excuses, blaming others for his problems, and overestimating the size of his enemy's forces. McClellan was not good at taking his troops into battle, or pursuing the enemy vigorously when McClellan had the advantage.

Thus, Lincoln fired him, because that is what good leaders do when they are operating a success-oriented enterprise.

What about us? Are we more like Lincoln or McClellan? Do we get things done and make things happen, or do we look good while accomplishing little and pointing in every direction to deflect blame? These questions really matter given that we are "co-laborers with Christ."

Are we really even trying to make a difference in a world full of people who are going to Hell without the Gospel, or are we content to make excuses?

We need to pray for a Great Awakening, and it needs to start inside us.

Day 78

November 11

Isaiah 9:6 "For a Child will be born for us, a Son will be given to us, and the government will be on His shoulders. He will be named Wonderful Counselor, Mighty God, Eternal Father, Prince of Peace."

Woodrow Wilson

Democratic Party

Peace

November 11 is commemorated as Veterans' Day in the United States. It's a day when the country celebrates all those who have served in the Armed Forces.

Before it was Veterans' Day, November 11 was known as Armistice Day because on that day in 1918, the Germans agreed to an armistice, or cease fire, which brought World War One to an end. It took President Woodrow Wilson quite some time, working with other world leaders, to put together a series of peace treaties. Even with all the time and effort, peace was shattered less than two decades later with the start of World War Two. The leaders of the world thought they could bring together their wisdom and power and create an everlasting peace after what they called "the War to End all Wars." But they could not get it done.

Many of us are content to hope and pray for a temporary cease fire with the things that stress and/or worry us. We settle for a peace that is only fleeting. This was already mentioned in a July devotion, but the lack of peace in our lives is so great that the topic warrants being mentioned again.

We need to put our hope in the Prince of Peace and not in our circumstances. This is a choice we must make day by day and hour after hour.

Day 79

November 12

Matthew 25:21 "His master said to him, 'Well done, good and faithful servant! You were faithful over a few things; I will put you in charge of many things. Share your master's joy."

George Washington

No Party Affiliation

Grit

George Washington became a high-ranking officer in the Virginia militia when he was barely into his twenties. He got this opportunity because he was good friends with a very rich and influential man.

It might be tempting to roll our eyes and say, "Yeah, it is all about who you know in life, and some people just get breaks that we don't." But it would be wrong to take that lesson from today's devotional thought.

November 12, 1694 is the day Augustine Washington was born. He was George's father. The elder Washington died in 1743. George was eleven years old. Losing his Dad was traumatic on an emotional level, as you can well imagine, and it also threw the family into economic turmoil. Formal schooling was cut short, which was another burden for a young man with ambition.

Washington could have felt sorry for himself. He could have lamented his sudden lack of options to move forward and become bitter. Instead, he learned a trade, land surveying, that was difficult back then but gave him the opportunity to get to know people of influence. And in his spare time he read books and practiced his handwriting.

Instead of engaging in self-pity over what he lacked, he showed plenty of grit, and he figured out how to maximize what he had.

We should pray that God would help us do the same today: display grit and figure out how to maximize our talents and resources.

Day 80

November 19

Mathew 28:19 "Go therefore, and make disciples of all nations, baptizing them in the name of the Father and of the Son and of the Holy Spirit."

James Garfield

Republican Party

Discipleship

James Garfield was born on this day in 1831, and he was unique. He fought for his country during the Civil War. He was the first left-handed President, which might not be legitimately special, but for some people it is an interesting piece of trivia. He was the second President to be assassinated, which is not special at all, but it is—thankfully—rare.

Garfield is the only President of the United States to be a minister. He was a member of the Disciples of Christ denomination, and on a part-time basis he preached and performed weddings and funerals.

He was highly regarded as a preacher and strongly implied that his work in that capacity was more significant than his job as President.

Some of the things we do are important. Some of our jobs directly and meaningfully impact the lives of others. Some of us are looking after children or other family members. But is there anything we can do today that is more important than loving God and sharing that love of God with others? Such work has an impact not only for this life, but for all eternity.

We need to communicate Christ.

We need to do it today.

Day 81

November 22A

I Corinthians 3:5-7 "What then is Apollos? What is Paul? They are servants through whom you believed, and each has the role the Lord has given. I planted, Apollos watered, but God gave the growth. So then neither the one who plants nor the one who waters is anything, but only God who gives the growth."

John Kennedy

Democratic Party

Hope

On this day in 1963, John Kennedy was assassinated. He left behind a wife and young children who would have to carry on without him. There was also the loss to the country of a Chief Executive who had done promising things and was poised to perhaps do many more.

He had shown bravery and compassion in not giving up on the people of West Berlin in a confrontation with the Soviets. He demonstrated intestinal fortitude in again confronting the Soviets over nuclear missiles in Cuba. Interestingly, despite such tensions, Kennedy negotiated a nuclear test ban treaty with the Soviets (and the British). He nudged things forward a little in the area of legal protection and fairness for African Americans. Kennedy pushed a tax cut through Congress that helped spur the economy.

Thus, Kennedy did things that pleased many different types of people in America. What more could he have accomplished with 5 more years in office (assuming he got reelected)? Kennedy was not perfect, no President is, but he had a string of successes with the opportunity for more—until he was assassinated.

Placing our hope in a politician is not the worst thing in the world (um, sometimes), but we need to remember that politicians can only do so much, and their time on the center stage is finite. And so it is with any earthly hero. As believers in Christ, we need to put our ultimate hope in Him. Our mood and outlook should not be victims of the temporary fortunes of men and women, no matter how powerful or successful they are in the moment.

Day 82

November 22B

Matthew 14:28-30 "'Lord, if it's You,' Peter answered Him, 'command me to come to You on the water.' He said, 'Come.' After climbing out of the boat, Peter started walking on the water and came toward Jesus. But when he saw the strength of the wind, he was afraid, and beginning to sink he cried out, 'Lord, save me!'"

Lyndon Johnson

Democratic Party

Decisions

After John Kennedy was assassinated on this day in 1963, Lyndon Johnson became the 36th President. Generally, historians praise Johnson for his handling of Civil Rights, and they bad mouth him for his handling of Vietnam. When it comes to social programs, what historians say has as much to do with their politics as his policies (liberals like his record, conservatives don't).

What's the takeaway? Well, LBJ made some great decisions and some terrible ones, which makes him a lot like all the rest of us. Such a reality should give us hope and humility. When it comes to the choices we make today, we need to realize that just because we have made bad/selfish/sinful/self-indulgent decisions in the past, it doesn't mean we are still locked into behaving that way. With the power of the Holy Spirit, we can change. Conversely, we should recognize that smart decisions yesterday do not make us invulnerable to bad decisions today. We are not too good or too smart or too spiritual to sin. Our spiritual victories and accomplishments don't put us outside the reach of temptation or sin. We have strengths, and we have weaknesses. The Holy Spirit can work through both our victories and our failures, but it would be nice if we asked Him for guidance as we experience both.

Day 83

November 23

I Corinthians 9:24 "Don't you know that the runners in a stadium all race, but only one receives the prize? Run in such a way to win the prize."

Franklin Pierce

Democratic Party

Quitting

On this day in 1804, Franklin Pierce was born. Twelve years later, he lived through something he never forgot. His father had sent him to boarding school in Hancock, New Hampshire, twelve miles from home. Young Pierce soured on his academic arrangements and one Sunday decided to walk home.

He was surprised at his father's subdued reaction upon seeing him. They enjoyed a quiet afternoon and a leisurely family dinner, then his father told him to get his things; Franklin was going back to school.

His father took him back in the family's carriage. Well, actually, his father took him part of the way back, then invited Franklin to get out and walk the rest of the way, carrying his heavy suitcase.

It was cold on that Sunday evening.

It was also raining.

Franklin Pierce learned a hard lesson about not quitting that night. And that lesson helped take him all the way to the White House after winning the Election of 1852.

Sometimes in life doors are closed, and there is nothing we can do about it. But there are other times when we are tempted to give up, despite whatever commitments we might have made. Our witness is more effective if our word is reliable.

We need to pray for wisdom as to when and where we make our commitments, but we also need to pray for the fortitude to not be quitters.

Day 84

December 2

Isaiah 40:31 "But those who trust in the Lord will renew their strength; they will soar on wings like eagles; they will run and not grow weary, they will walk and not faint."

Theodore Roosevelt

Republican Party

Hope

On this day in 1886, Theodore Roosevelt married his second wife, Edith. This was more than two years after the death of his first wife, Alice, which was covered in the February 14 devotion. Teddy and Edith, childhood friends, eventually had five kids together and were quite happy. This is a sweet ending to what started out as a tragic story.

Sometimes in life we experience a setback from which we do not think we will recover, and then with the passage of time we experience an unexpected blessing. One might be tempted to think, "Yeah, it's like when people say, 'When God closes a door, He opens a window.'" But one shouldn't say that because doors and windows serve different functions.

One might be tempted to reply, "It's like when God says 'no' to one thing you've asked for, and it's because there is a bigger blessing right around the corner." Unfortunately, that is not always true in the context in which it is offered. Sometimes you don't get hired for the job you've applied for, but it doesn't always mean you'll get a better job. Sometimes God doesn't heal your sick loved one, and it doesn't mean He is going to send someone into your life that you will love just as much, even though that kind of happened with Roosevelt.

God might bless us with something better than what we've asked, but sometimes He doesn't. Here is the bigger truth for today: Christians will be blessed when we leave this world to such an extent that all of our hardships will seem like nothing. This is where we place our hope as believers—not in our circumstances in this life, but in the blessings that are to come in Heaven.

Day 85

December 5

John 5:17 "Jesus responded to them, 'My Father is still working, and I am working also.'"

Martin Van Buren

Democratic Party

Trust

On this day in 1782, Martin Van Buren was born. This might seem like ~~useless~~ ~~trivia~~* something only historians would care about, but the circumstances of Van Buren's birth are significant to him, to American history, and to our devotional today. His father was a tavern owner, and young Martin was the 4th of 9 children. With only a modest income from the tavern, and so many mouths to feed, financial resources were stretched thin.

Rather than generating feelings of sorrow for Van Buren, these circumstances were blessings that were keys to the success of the man who became the 8th President of the United States. Growing up poor, and being frustrated by it, spurred Van Buren to create lofty goals for himself. Being a middle child taught Van Buren how to compromise and get along with different kinds of people. The tavern served as a polling place at election time, and it was always a gathering spot for the men in the community who talked about what was going on in their world. Thus, the tavern introduced Van Buren to the political realm and to the wants and needs of the citizenry. Van Buren processed all this and figured out how to use it to his advantage.

Likewise, today we find ourselves in our own unique set of circumstances. There are frustrations in our lives, but what if they are God's way of teaching us something? We should pray for wisdom today. We should pray that God would show us how to turn at least one of our frustrations to our advantage. And His.

*This was not careless editing; I just think the strikethrough function is funny.

Day 86

December 7

Esther 7:10 "They hanged Haman on the gallows he had prepared for Mordecai. Then the king's anger subsided."

Franklin Roosevelt

Democratic Party

Wisdom

On this day in 1941, of course, the Japanese engaged in a sneak attack on Pearl Harbor and other American bases in the Pacific, killing about 2400 Americans and damaging many of our planes and ships. Franklin Roosevelt said it was a day that would live in infamy, and he called on Congress to declare war.

The Japanese were not trying to conquer the United States; they were trying to force us to resume trading with them, which we had cut off because we did not want to support Japan's efforts to conquer their neighbors.

Obviously, Japan's plan backfired. We did not resume trade with them in the short term; we went to war. And we ended that war with some atomic bombs.

Like the Japanese in this scenario, many times we Christians rationalize actions that hurt someone else. Maybe it's a situation at work; maybe it's a family thing. We try not to focus on the harm we're doing, as we direct our attention to why we need to do it to help ourselves. But there is a different King we answer to, and His anger is something we definitely do not want to provoke. Haman was a man with a lot of authority and power. He felt justified in plotting something unpleasant for Mordecai. Do you have a lot of power at work or in your family? Pray for wisdom as you wield that power today.

Day 87

December 14

Joshua 1:1 "After the death of Moses the LORD's servant, the LORD spoke to Joshua son of Nun."

George Washington

No Party Affiliation

Leadership

On this day in 1799, George Washington died. He was a hero of the French and Indian War, the biggest hero of the American Revolution, the presiding official at the Constitutional Convention, and President of the United States for the first eight years of the new government. But on December 14, 1799, he passed away.

For those of us who have been around long enough, we have experienced the loss of a great leader/mentor in our lives.

Some of us are reluctant to step up and fill a leadership void. But the wheel keeps turning, and new leaders are needed, ready or not.

We say we're not ready, but neither was Washington at first. Joshua might not have felt like he was prepared to be the next Moses. As it turned out, the Israelites did not need a second Moses, they needed a first Joshua.

There was a leadership void when Washington passed away, and it was filled. They were all different from him, but they stepped up. They were not perfect—Adams was irritating, Jefferson was dishonest, Madison was low key even when boldness was called for. But they were great in other ways, and perhaps most importantly of all, they were willing to serve. We can do the same.

Day 88

December 22

Luke 23:34 "Then Jesus said, 'Father, forgive them, because they do not know what they are doing.' And they divided His clothes and cast lots."

Andrew Jackson

Democratic Party

Forgiveness

On this sad day in 1828, Rachel Jackson, beloved wife of the 7th President, died. She had a bad heart, and the Election of 1828, one of the ugliest in American history, was too much for her. Political adversaries pointed out that she was still married to her first husband when she wed Andrew Jackson. It was a humiliating revelation on a national scale for a quiet woman who had decided to live for Christ during one of America's Great Awakenings.

The exact timeline of her journey as a bigamist isn't relevant here, but she was guilty as charged, and thoroughly embarrassed when this skeleton was pulled out of her closest and put on display. When she first heard reports that this story was being circulated, she fainted on the spot. She died just a few weeks later, which led Andrew Jackson and others to attribute her death to the stress of the scandal.

Andrew Jackson was a highly volatile man who was quick to take things personally. He went to his grave believing that mean politics killed his wife. Forgiveness did not come easy to him. He genuinely loved his wife, and hated his political opponents with a passion.

We have all been hurt. We all know forgiveness is ideal. There are many of us, however, who have a limit beyond which we will not forgive.

Thank God, He didn't feel the same about us. Christ, who was perfectly innocent, was tortured to death for our sin. He forgave us even though we totally did not deserve it. That is who we are called to forgive—those who do not deserve it.

The path of the Christian is so hard sometimes. But the reward is worth it!

Day 89

December 25

Luke 2:6-7 "While they were there, the time came for her (Mary) to give birth. Then she gave birth to her firstborn Son, and she wrapped Him tightly in cloth and laid Him in a manger, because there was no guest room available for them."

Franklin Pierce

Democratic Party

Benjamin Harrison

Republican Party

Christmas

Merry Christmas! Here's a trivia question that might be more interesting than you realize: Who was the first President to put up a Christmas tree in the White House? Some say it was our 14th President, Franklin Peirce, but others insist it was number 23, Benjamin Harrison.

Doesn't it seem like we should know that definitively? Pierce took office in 1853—we have pretty good records from back then.

Maybe it's for the best in our balkanized (polarized) world that historians cannot decide who should get the credit, the Democrat or the Republican.

Whichever it was, it is nice that Christmas was recognized in the White House in such a public way.

As Christians, we see Christmas as the celebration of God's great gift to us: Jesus, Who came to Earth to sacrifice Himself for our salvation. We do not have to content ourselves with celebrating this just one time a year. We can embrace this hope and joy every day. Pierce and Harrison brought Christmas into the White House. We need to take Christmas out into the world.

Joy to the world!

Day 90

December 28

I Peter 5:6-7 "Humble yourselves, therefore, under the mighty hand of God, so that He may exalt you at the proper time, casting all your cares on Him, because He cares for you."

Thomas Jefferson

Democratic-Republican Party

Peace

On this day in 1790, Thomas Jefferson issued a report. He was not yet President; he was serving as the first secretary of state under George Washington. In Jefferson's report, he wrote about men having instructions from Congress regarding how to handle pirates operating out of North Africa. The problem, Jefferson wrote, was that the fast-changing situation rendered the instructions obsolete. The men representing the US had to improvise.

This kind of dynamic can be stressful in our lives, too. We have a plan to deal with a situation at home, at work, at church, or wherever, then life throws us a curveball. Jefferson's people had to deal with Muslim pirates who had no moral qualms about capturing merchant sailors and holding them for ransom. (I mentioned the faith of the pirates because they rationalized their behavior at the time by saying they only kidnapped infidels [those they perceived to be Christians], so the pirates said their behavior was not sinful.)

We don't face stress like that, but the stresses that we do face seem overwhelming enough at times. This is when our faith can really shine! When we can maintain an attitude of peace in times where common sense would dictate stress and worry, what a powerful witness that is.

Peace has been a recurring theme in this book, because the lack of it is a recurring problem in our hearts. We should pray for peace today. If we are at peace, it shows that our faith is genuine. We need that.

The world needs to see that.

About the Author

Timothy D. Holder is a professor of History at Walters State Community College where he is also an assistant dean, and he is an ordained minister. With a Ph. D. and Masters in History, and a Masters in Applied Theology to go along with a BA in Bible, Holder's two lifelong fields of study, his two passions, come together in *Presidential Stories*. He and his wife, Angela, live in Knoxville, Tennessee.

Other Books by the Author

Presidential Character: George Washington through John Quincy Adams

Presidential Trivia 2.0

Made in the USA
Lexington, KY
08 December 2018